Dollars for Excellence

Dollars for Excellence

Roy K. Bunce and Stanton Leggett

Teach 'em, Chicago, Illinois

Library of Congress Catalog Card Number:
87-51102

International Standard Book Number:
0-931028-97-3

Teach 'em, Inc.
160 East Illinois Street
Chicago, Illinois 60611

92 91 90 89 88   5 4 3 2 1

Printed in the United States of America

Contents

Prologue

Why should the board of education carry on a fund raising campaign in its community when it has the power to raise taxes to get the money it needs?

This is a sensible question and there are a number of sensible answers. Careful consideration of the question suggests that the board of education should gear up and designate fund raising as a major function of the board.

The reasons: The school system has always raised money for some of its needs, perhaps not at the scale anticipated here, but there is a tradition and experience in soliciting gifts for the schools and for some of the programs the tax based budget will not support. Raising the tax rate to meet legitimate educational needs is getting more difficult and, in some cases, is not allowed by laws that place caps or severe restrictions upon tax rate increases. Perhaps the most important reason is that the act of seeking voluntary contributions of money to improve the quality of the school system is in itself a significant contribution to the quality of the system.

The fact that the schools have for many years developed a tradition of seeking private money to help support school programs is almost universally demonstrated. The principal function of PTA or PTO organizations in most schools has been to raise money to buy a computer, or decorate a room, or purchase books for the library. Band parents have helped with the support of band travel or the purchase of uniforms. Publications have been financed with advertisements solicited from merchants in the community. Cake sales, admissions, and similar activities all have strong adherents as tools for securing additional funds. This book details the ways in which sporadic and short term efforts in fund raising can become significant, long term in nature, and powerful in effect.

Our current national posture has emphasized the role of tax increases as a measure of last resort. When such a general attitude, reinforced by spending caps and other restrictions on the power to tax, comes in conflict with the desire of a community to improve the quality of its schools, solicitation of private money may be the only alternative. This is a hard fact for publicly supported institutions to face. Yet state universities have strong development offices. These institutions have accepted the necessity for reaching both to the public tax system and to private philanthropy to provide the service its constituency wants.

Most public school board members do not look upon themselves as elected to take on the responsibility of proper financial support of the school system. Most school administrators are highly skilled at the process of gaining support for tax increases or tax levies or budget increases. When these traditional funding sources are closed off, new skills must be learned and new roles accepted both by the board of education or school committee members and by their professional school administrators.

In addition to the general swing away from taxes as a solution to financing problems, there has been a substantial demographic change. The baby boom population has had its children at a much reduced rate. As a result, in many communities a surprisingly small percentage of the general population have children in public schools. Although education has usually received favorable treatment from voters over the long haul, the core of the support for school levies and budgets has been parents with immediate interests in supporting the schools educating their children. The shrinking of this loyal support group diminishes the power of the board of education and its administrators to influence the size of the public school budget. As these factors play out in front of the board of education, there will arise new willingness to consider alternative methods of financing the schools.

Perhaps the most important reason for undertaking a full fledged campaign of fund raising for the public schools will be to gain not only money but also the joint involvement of board members, school staff, and community in significant ways to improve the quality of education in the schools. Taxes are impersonal and are difficult to get enthusiastic about. When one makes even a small gift to a cause, there is an identification with that cause, a sense of investment in something that to you is most worthwhile. When staff members see community members as potential investors in the work of the school there is a difference in attitude. Taxpayers, once the vote is carried, have little choice. In contrast, investors can add or subtract from their gift, can become ardent supporters of programs, and can persuade others to invest. The day-to-day contact with such supporters by the school staff changes the way the staff involves the investors, helps indicate to the school some of the visions in which givers are willing to invest, and performs a bonding effect upon teachers and supporters that spells a new high in morale and mutual respect. Fund raising is one powerful way to capitalize on the worth of the school to the community.

Schools, asked to perform better, with many ways blocked to obtain more tax support, and a tradition of low level fund raising efforts, can readily move to systematic, carefully conceived methods of raising funds from their constituencies. Although money will be the result, one of the great advantages of a fund raising campaign will be the shoulder-to-shoulder work of board of education members, staff, teachers, parents, and concerned members of the community in improving the quality of education.

Introduction

Private fund raising for public schools has in some states nearly achieved the status of a movement. In community after community one can witness the set up of public education foundations at the district level and other vehicles to receive funds from the private sector.

When groups consider fund raising from the private sector, they should first look at the current sources of giving. In 1986 the American family contributed approximately $87 billion to a wide range of charities from religion to health to general community services. Of that $83.5 billion, 79 percent was provided by living individuals in the form of gifts from income and/or personal assets. An additional 11 percent was provided to charities through individuals' wills or estate plans. Corporations provided 5 percent of the American charitable dollar; foundations provided a larger amount.

This reality forces all institutions to face the fact that foundations and corporations will never be able to pick up completely the unmet needs and resources. When one compares dollars given for special projects versus annual support, the predominance of individual giving becomes more marked. The largest potential in annual fund raising today lies in the charity of individuals. Therefore, while we will include sections on foundation and corporate solicitation, this book will primarily focus on methods to secure support from individuals through gifts given during their lifetimes as well as those donated through estate plans and wills.

Fund raising is never an end in itself. Without a cause, it is lifeless. A vision must exist for any fund raising program to work. This vision is the blood of fund raising. Volunteers are the body. Dreams and visions for our public schools that come alive will raise dollars more than any other single factor.

Important in any effort to raise money are the attitudes with which one approaches the solicitation. A common misconception is that fund raising is a distasteful, manipulative, coercive activity that extracts money from unwilling participants—the rich. Effective fund raising never involves any of the above. Instead, it presents to the individual donor a vision of how he or she can fulfill personal goals in a way that individuals could not accomplish alone: In this case, through a contribution to the local school district.

Three words should never occur in a fund raising program—should, ought, or could. It is never the solicitor's responsibility to tell the prospective donor what he or she should do, ought to do, or can do. That's the responsibility of the donor. The solicitor is the vehicle for the transmission of a vision of what "could be" if everyone pulls together in a meaningful response to the needs of our public schools.

Effective fund raising can only be accomplished by people. It cannot be automated. Asking and giving are both personal experiences. Fund raising can only be performed when someone takes the lead.

Fund raising is a learned skill. It is different from sales, in the ordinary sense of the word, yet it is a breed of selling. Fund raising is similar in function to the activities of brokers and manufacturers' representatives who match specific needs with products or present investors with an opportunity to fulfill their individual goals.

Fund raising must grow out of a school district's broad, long term goals and current programs. When this is the case and a school district's constituencies clearly understand what must be accomplished, they will give their support.

Fund raising, if it is to be successful on a long term basis, must be a part of a total institutional advancement program that includes public relations, publications, and constituency relations.

Let us now look at types of fund raising currently in use. Fund raising divides into two basic categories: event- and donor-centered fund raising. Event-centered programming is where the "prospect" buys a ticket or pays to participate in an event or persuades sponsors to back his walk-a-thon, ski-a-thon, or other "thon." Event-centered fund raising views potential donors as a market to be developed. Donor-centered fund raising emphasizes individual solicitation; a process where people ask their neighbors for gifts to support a common cause. In this case, the donor is a friend of the cause rather than an impersonal "market." Donor-centered fund raising can be aptly called "friend-raising."

The following is a point by point comparison of event- and donor-centered fund raising which will highlight differences between the two.

Donor education

Event-centered	Donor-centered
• Programs focus on an activity such as a telethon, a casino night, or a recognition dinner. The emphasis is on the featured activity, not the needs of the school district. There is very little learning about the district's needs and long term goals.	• A continuous learning process about the public schools takes place. The more the donors know, the more they are likely to give.

continued

Event-centered	Donor-centered
• Donors quickly forget that they contributed to a cause rather than bought a ticket.	• An informed, educated donor can see that his or her individual contribution has made a difference because of the constant communication between solicitor and donor. The gift is remembered because the donor gets a positive feeling from giving.
• Events produce little involvement with the district's schools because there is a paucity of information beyond a printed entertainment program. The base of support is unchanged and if another competing event has more appeal next year, the constituency may desert you.	• After learning about their schools, donors become more involved as their commitment deepens, producing a broad base of constant support.

Donor involvement

Event-centered	Donor-centered
• People buy a ticket for their own amusement.	• People make an investment in a better tomorrow.
• There is little carry-over from the event to the cause of the school district because the vital issues are obscured by the event. If they find something more entertaining next year, prospects will not show up.	• Prospects are insiders with a personal stake in the outcome of a fund raising program. The emphasis is on developing relationships with those whose personal values and sense of community support the goals of the school district.

Income potential

Event-centered	Donor-centered
• There is a built-in ceiling on earnings because only so many people will fit in an auditorium. There is often a limit on how much you can charge above what would normally be the price for commercial entertainment or activities.	• The ceiling is as high as the goals you set, and there is no space requirement. How much is given depends on the donor's ability to give, not on the price of a night out. There is never a competing event because fund raising is continuous and convenient to donor.

Event-centered	Donor-centered
• The donor is asked to give an average amount keyed to the lowest common denominator. While some dinners and other events which focus on a specific rather than general population audience offer participation at various levels of giving there is seldom an effective effort to match asking with potential.	• The "asking" is keyed to the institution's need, the donor's ability to give, and the donor's level of commitment/involvement.
• "Thons"—ski-a-thons, skate-a-thons, etc.—have a specific time period after which they are ineffective. The event must be changed if the seasonal deadline is missed.	• The weather and season do not make any difference. Individual solicitation continues all year long.
• The success of the event is often linked with the personality of one or two individuals in leadership positions at that time. If the leadership changes, the event often must as well.	• Fund raising goes on regardless of who happens to be in a specific position of leadership. A change at the top has little effect because the institution, not someone's event, is the focus.

Program management

Event-centered	Donor-centered
• Management is riveted to the event itself and the time and place are determined by the event. It is a mass marketing venture with little distinction among individual prospects. It is a "one shot" gamble for donor dollars.	• The program management is flexible in terms of time and place because it boils down to one person asking another in a convenient situation. The cultivation, asking, and solicitation can be tailored to the knowledge and attitudes of the individual prospect. Some will take longer to "buy in" than others.

SECTION ONE—

A fund raising overview: What is behind the program?

1   The first, the few, and the committed

If you are the first in your community to read a book such as this and consider the pros and cons of raising funds for your public school, do not be disheartened. As we have indicated, public schools have been raising money from the private sector for quite some time. You are not really alone. It is only the scope of your vision that sets you apart. Remember that fund raiser where parents and others concerned with public education collected enough money to buy a computer or a film projector for the auditorium? The money came from those sympathetic to that particular project.

But now, with local budgets getting thin, it is time to think about the long term goals schools should be setting. Instead of trying to raise money for an isolated cause (e.g. a computer) the situation is fast arising where it will be necessary to go to the private sector for financial help on a larger scale.

The private sector comprises personal friends as well as the friends of the community's schools. These individuals can provide the funds to make sure schools continue to move toward the educational excellence our children will need to survive and prosper.

Chapter One focuses on you—the first to envision what

our public schools can be with the help of additional funds. It also focuses on those to whom this vision must be communicated, namely the school board and the board of directors of a new fund raising foundation. Raising the funds from the private sector, which will increase and perpetuate the strengths of our public schools, is definitely possible because it is not an altogether novel idea.

Nearly all not-for-profit institutions, whether historically funded by public or private dollars, enjoy support from both sources of revenue. Institutions of the arts, sciences, and humanities receive appropriations from local, state, and federal governments. At the same time they seek and receive gifts from individuals, private foundations, and corporate patrons.

The needs of the poor, the elderly, and the very young, as well as the health needs of the general community are met through a complex of parallel and often interdependent delivery systems and institutions each sponsored by public and private dollars.

Higher education, both private and public, regularly receives operating dollars as well as special project funding from both private contributors and public grants. Indeed, the only major institutions in America that are not sustained by funding from both sectors are the judicial system, the military, churches, and local public school systems.

The public's notion of what constitutes appropriate funding sources has changed over the years. The congregations of New England worshiped in publicly supported town halls long before they became all those white clapboard churches. Many of today's public schools have their roots in private academies and many were for years sustained by a dual support system.

In the last fifteen years many private secondary schools have been receiving federal and state support through lunch programs, transportation, textbook subsidies and programs for the gifted and handicapped. Looking back only a few years, one can read of battles in the state legislatures over whether it was appropriate for a state university to add a public relations office to its administration. A couple years ago, five of the twenty top fund raising universities in America were public institutions.

Attitudes concerning what constitutes appropriate support for local school districts can also change. But what is the first step? How does one begin?

Because fund raising on this scale is a new idea there are few public school models that have been in existence long enough to serve as a guide for others. In addition, school districts are subject to such a variety of circumstances that each program must be tailored to meet a particular set of needs. Therefore let's look first at some of the more generic issues to be faced. Here are fifteen points to ponder when beginning a program in private fund raising.

1) One is the loneliest number

Be prepared to start alone. You will face a certain amount of hostility and rejection. But even more, anticipate encountering inertia—a formidable obstacle to success. Please remember: successful fund raising programs begin in the mind of one person who takes the idea to a few more people until finally a common goal is set and achieved.

2) It takes time to change minds

Anticipate a long period of consciousness raising. For most, fund raising is a new idea. Don't expect immediate acceptance. It will take time for people to warm to the idea of private funding for public schools.

3) Good times, not crises, raise big bucks

Good times, not crises, provide the best ambience for soliciting voluntary contributions. The tax dollar responds to need—it is given out of obligation. The charitable dollar responds to vision—it is an investment. Asking for support in times of crisis forces the root question, "What shall we do?" to share the stage with the question, "Who allowed this crisis to develop?" Is it the result of mismanagement? People give more generously when supporting excellence than when repairing a leak.

4) Paint the picture by the numbers

Prepare your "case" for support *before* speaking with others. How will you spend additional funds? How essential is additional funding to fulfilling the goals of the district? How essential will it be in five years? Keep it positive. Clearly explain what will be accomplished when the needs are met. The strongest case for support will contain:

1. The institution's track record: its history, its roots, its heritage.
2. A clear statement of today's needs.
3. A statement of what has already been done to meet the need.
4. A clear picture of the solution.
5. An indication of what others are doing to implement the solution.
6. A clear statement of what is needed from the prospective donor to complete the goal.

5) Plans, not questions, provide the strongest openings

When speaking with others, do *not* lead with "How do you feel about private funding for public schools?" That is like asking, "How do you feel about living with one kidney?" before explaining that a brother or a sister may die without a transplant.

Individuals must have a complete picture of needs and possible solutions before they can make a considered response to any situation. Offer individuals a plan, not a question: a vision, not simply a need.

6) Nothing succeeds like . . .

Begin by talking with many individuals before bringing a group together. Success breeds success so begin where there is a special reason for, or demonstration of, commitment:

    a. Parents of students specially served.

    b. Parent volunteers already involved in school functions.

    c. Alumni or business people living in the community who are vocally supportive of your programs.

7) Make your odds overwhelming

When convening a group/committee, blatantly stack the deck. Build a base of supportive citizens and then let them answer the questions of others. The role of the elected board and district administration is to instigate not initiate fund raising.

8) A new governance for a new day

Volunteer leadership outside the elected school board and district administration will be required for success. The school board is elected to supervise and manage the resources provided by the electing body—not to insure income. Some board members will also become effective solicitors for the public schools but many will not. Therefore, consider establishing a separate nonprofit foundation to solicit, receive, and disperse funds for strengthening the public schools. This foundation should include volunteer members of the community and should be governed by a self-perpetuating board of trustees who coordinate with the school board to respond to the needs of the district.

9) Private support is a well that never runs dry

The charitable dollar has waxed and waned, as has the tax dollar, depending more upon demonstrated need than fluctuating affluence. Both stem from that portion of an individual's resources beyond those needed for survival. Individuals invest their resources in projects they find monetarily rewarding or personally fulfilling. The local schools can provide such a meaningful investment opportunity.

10) Count no one out

Do not exclude any potential donors from your thinking. As noted 90 percent of the billions of dollars donated each year is given by living individuals. Ten percent is donated through wills. Five percent is provided by corporations and 5 percent by foundations. Alumni, so well cultivated by the private school, are often overlooked as a loyal, concerned constituency who can be mobilized as a supportive force. Cultivation and involvement, not genetics, make the private school alumnus so loyal and generous.

11) Spread the leadership around

Responsibility for the program must be in the hands of volunteers enlisted from each constituency group you hope to reach. Committed volunteers who have made their own gift make the best solicitors. The first volunteer board determines the success of the first year's activities. It must provide not only leadership in work and wisdom, but leadership in making contributions as well.

12) Set realistic goals

Goals must be attainable yet provide a challenge commensurate with the constituency's ability and willingness to respond. For best results, goals should be set after conducting a feasibility study to determine potential. In most situations it should be anticipated that the volunteer board will provide 25-50 percent of the dollars through the start-up years. While goals are accomplished year to year, projections should be made for three to five years. This can also amortize the high start-up cost and relatively low income one should anticipate in the first one to two years.

This book is primarily concerned with developing an annual fund: a program designed to solicit modest but annual gifts from a broad base of donors that will establish a firm pattern of giving to public education. Once set, the annual fund will provide the base for future capital campaigns— the program through which one generally receives the larger gift.

13) It takes money to raise money

Anticipate realistic costs. Development programs in private schools with 1,000 to 2,000 donors can carry significant cost. Initial expenses can be kept lower, but adequate budget for staff and program is essential to providing support to the volunteer structure.

Although the program need not be lavish, to spend too little (under capitalize the program, and so forth) can mean it would have been better to have done nothing at all.

14) Is there a price to success?

If the campaign is successful, will the donor want to run the school? Not if it is already well run. Unlike the taxpayer who tends to say, "I have paid the fee, now produce," the donor generally seeks a greater personal involvement. But donors have jobs, families, and other activities and they generally do not have the time to run the school. In fact, the volunteer board of the private school has much less involvement in the daily operations of its institution than does the elected school board in the district's activities.

15) If at first you don't succeed . . .

Rejection provides another piece of data that is needed to achieve success. Do not be discouraged if everyone you speak to does not agree with your insight. Use their comments to refine your approach and keep going.

The opportunities for providing private funding for public schools are limitless but the process requires planning and commitment. Any fund raising effort must be conscientiously supported over the years to flourish. The need for such an effort is becoming increasingly apparent as some communities are forced to cut important programs and others struggle to maintain their standards of excellence.

Private fund raising is certain to play a growing role in the school yards and classrooms of America's public schools. Those with the vision and commitment to initiate a fund raising program can reap rewards of a substantial nature: the knowledge that the schools may continue to promote excellence, and the nourishment of the students who are our country's future.

2 Identifying those who care

A crucial initial step in fund raising is identifying the various groups of people who have an interest in seeing the goals of the institution met. These groups make up the constituencies that will be informed, involved, and solicited during the fund raising program.

Broadly speaking, three types of relationships between a school and the public define the major constituent groupings within a community: 1) Those who are or have been users of the public schools, 2) those who depend on the health of the public schools for their own financial well being and, 3) those who have a history of providing support for public education.

It is relatively easy to identify those who use the public schools: alumni, parents, and others who have a place within the facility or programs there.

It is a common misconception that public school alumni cannot be cultivated like their private school counterparts to develop a feeling of loyalty toward their alma mater. In most cases, school loyalty is not to the institution per se but to the experiences, shared with peers and teachers, that have molded the student during the years of growth. Alumni often view former teachers and schoolmates as having a lot to do with making them what they are today.

The relationships initiated during these formative years, therefore, have the potential to develop into lifelong friendships if there is a vehicle to keep alumni in touch with each other and the school. This is a case where public schools might follow the lead of private educational institutions. Such activities as homecoming festivities, already a part of many public school programs, can serve the purpose of maintaining contact.

To get started, alumni who care must first be identified and located. One obvious way is to ask alumni parents for information about their children. Designating alumni as class agents to help in the search is another approach. A third basic method is to compare current telephone books with high school yearbooks to see who is living in the area. Community leaders, particularly doctors, lawyers, and other professionals who have returned to the area to practice, are often a font of information about classmates.

Publishing an alumni directory is an excellent tool for turning up alumni if it is coupled with a strong public relations effort urging former public school students to send in their addresses and other pertinent information.

If the public high school is a feeder institution for a local state or community college, the alumni affairs office of such institutions may be willing to share its lists of students recruited from your school. Also, never underestimate the potential of involving current students in the alumni search as part of a class project.

Parents also are among those who use the public schools. Already directly involved in the welfare of their schools, parent organizations raise significant amounts of money for programs and special projects such as the acquisition of movie projectors, universal gyms, and the like. Commendable as this is, a comparison with the contributions of private school parents reveals that the private school parents provide upward of 10 percent of the school's operating budget, and that contribution is given on top of a hefty tuition payment made after paying the same taxes public school parents pay to support public education.

A third group who increasingly use public schools are adults and senior citizens. The days when schools were for children only have long since passed. With decreasing enrollments, more resources are becoming available for general community use. As these citizens participate in programs they become prospects for an on-going fund raising program.

Although most people in a community depend either directly or indirectly on the health of the public schools, the most obvious group in this category are the vendors. Stronger educational programs mean more dollars spent locally. Moreover, community businesses depend on public schools for more than profit at the cash register. The small restauranteur, hardware store owner, and others are often dependent upon student labor for a good part of their labor force. Better quality students mean better business.

Homeowners too are dependent upon quality public schools to maintain the value of their investment. A recent headline in the *New York Times* real estate section read, "As Goes the Public School, So Goes the Cost of Homes." How many of us have moved into a specific community because of the caliber of the schools and paid more for housing than we would have in the next community? Virtually any individual living within the community is a prospective doner. All benefit in one way or another from a school district that provides a program of excellence.

The quality of a community's public schools also affects locally headquartered corporations, which are already paying a significant tax for local public education. National and multi-national corporations operating in the community pay an additional "tax" if the schools are not strong. Corporations are forced to pay executives more so they can send their children to private schools or bear the cost of a long commute.

Conversely, if the community currently enjoys strong public schools, how much more will a corporation have to pay if local schools begin to falter? Would it not be cheaper to make a contribution "up front" to prevent their demise? In identifying locally headquartered corporations that depend on the public schools, one should identify alumni currently employed by them.

Corporations encourage the support of private education, often basing their gift upon the number of individuals working for them who graduated from a given institution. This giving is most often done through matching gift programs—when employees donate to their alma mater the company matches it.

Businesses do this for private schools while ignoring the fact that 90 percent of their employees come from public schools. In fact, their policy often excludes secondary education altogether. Corporations tend to contribute to the college or university that refined their employee's skills and ignore the elementary and secondary schools that taught the basics.

Those who have a stated commitment to community causes such as public education can usually be identified. These include family foundations (similar in nature though not in scope to the Ford and Rockefeller Foundations), city or community foundations, resident corporate foundations and a limited number of national foundations. Many of these are controlled by a volunteer board made up of community leaders.

The key to identifying these potential prospects, particularly family and corporate foundations, is locating local bankers and lawyers who helped set them up and maintain them as executors or trustees. If these attorneys and financial experts are alumni and can be involved in a fund raising program, so much the better.

There are different patterns of giving between individuals and corporations or foundations. Each responds to a different type of appeal. Large organizations, such as corporations and foundations, respond best to one time gifts. Individuals, although they in some instances follow suit, often adopt the school district's cause in such a way that they will support it over a lengthy period of time.

The reason that corporate giving takes the form of a one-time-only donation (although the contribution may be repeated periodically) is that it is advantageous for the company to "buy" a program that can be closely identified with itself.

For instance, a large pharmaceutical manufacturer may prefer to donate $15,000 for a new chemistry laboratory in a local high school. This is also a way for a corporation to invest in what they know best: pharmaceutical companies donate laboratories, computer firms give funds for personal computers. There is an advantage for public school fund raisers in all of this too. Corporations and foundations, with their propensity for periodically giving larger sums, are invaluable as a source of start-up and special project funding.

A typical giving pattern might be to concentrate on corporate donations for the initial costs in a fund raising effort until individual donors sustain the program. Of course, the corporate and foundation funding sources can be tapped for a special capital project, but it is the individual donor who provides the continuous flow of funds.

There is danger in depending on a corporate or foundation donor for continuous support. Sooner or later support wanes due to a change in attitude or the death of a key person within that organization. In general ask the large corporate and foundation donors for initial funding and special projects. Rely on individuals for a constant influx of funds.

3 Qualifying/rating those who care

How much do you need from me? How much are others giving? How much do I need to give as an individual to insure
success? All these questions live in the mind of the donor.
The solicitor who prepares to answer these questions often
determines the quality of the solicitation experience and
the size of the gift.

As the old saying goes, "You never get more than you ask
for." But, how much do you ask for? Although the answer is
not easy, there is one. It lies among a number of factors: the
ability of the individual to give, the total need of the institution, the giving patterns of the institution's supporters of
the past, the anticipated scale of gifts needed to accomplish
current goals.

Establishing proper institutional goals is the beginning of
the development of an individual asking plan. The goal for
a specific campaign starts with the needs of the institution
and should grow out of an articulate and thorough long-
range planning process. Any effective long-range planning
includes the question: How much money do we need to accomplish the goals we have set for ourselves? Institutional
needs alone cannot determine the goal, for the objective
dollar need is modified by the institution's realistic chance
to raise those dollars.

Goal setting often goes on for days, weeks, months, and sometimes even years. Usually final goals are not announced until the leadership of the program has had a chance to make its own pledges and demonstrate that it is able and willing to set a giving pattern to meet the goal. If leadership does not give, no dollar goal will be reached. The question now becomes: How much must the leadership give to accomplish the goal?

Donors do not give in average amounts. Their gift, in addition to being governed by their ability to give, is equally and perhaps more profoundly affected by their willingness to give. Willingness is based upon the individual's perception of the quality of the investment.

Does the institution have sound management and a program that is vital to the lives of people? Is the new need urgent enough for the prospect to take on a new level of giving? Is this cause more urgent than others? Will more be accomplished by contributing to the public schools than to other institutions that may be appealing to the prospect at the same time?

Although people do not give in average amounts, they give in similar patterns. Therefore, it is important to begin identifying the pattern or "scale of gifts" that will be essential to achieving the goal. A donation of $100,000 is not raised through 1000 individuals each giving $100. To raise $100,000 it is likely that some individuals are going to give gifts in excess of $2,500 or $3,000. Others will need to give in the range of $1,500 to $2,000, others in the range of $750 to $1,000, and so on down to the lowest dollar donor.

Such a scale of gifts is essential to the foundation trustees or campaign leadership when determining how much they must give to make the campaign successful. The key will be in the ability to distribute the scale of gifts appropriately across the prospective donor base with a specific asking that reflects the individual's ability and willingness to give.

The process of determining askings is not a process that indicates what the donor should or can give. Rather, it develops an asking that says: "It is hoped that you will consider a gift in the range of $___. If you and others like you will consider becoming one of the ___ number of donors needed to give in that range, we are sure we will find success."

What if the donor asks, "What is my share of $100,000?" The best answer would be a definition of the need as it translates to an individual's gift. This would leave the prospect with the confidence that if "I do my share, together we will be successful."

"Give all you can" is never an appropriate asking. Such a statement leaves the prospective donor with no better understanding of how the need applies to him or her as an individual than before the question was asked. When told to "give all you can," the prospect is left with no guidelines to help determine what an appropriate share might be. Leaving a solicitation open-ended generally means a smaller gift this year and makes next year's gift more difficult to acquire.

The final reason for the development of askings lies in the reality that peer solicitation is the most effective solicitation. Individuals should never be sent out on a call asking for more money than they themselves can give and have given.

How to develop appropriate askings

So how do we develop such an asking? The concept is a simple one. If you bring ten or twelve people into a room, hold up a string, and ask them to write down how long they think the string is, an analysis of their responses will reveal two facts. First, the person reading the responses will be amazed at how wrong some people are. Equally startling will be the high degree of accuracy reflected in the average of their responses. Qualifying individuals as major gift donors, lead gift donors, general donors, etc., is an equally subjective process, but it is also equally accurate.

Look at the scale of gifts and answer the questions, "If I had to ask five individuals to consider giving in the range of $2,500, who among our constituency would I ask?" and "If I had to ask 700 people to consider gifts in the range of $25, who among our constituency would I ask?"

The development of askings is a volunteer's problem. Volunteers know their peers' ability to give and their attitudes toward the institution.

To begin, ask your volunteer leadership to divide the current prospect base into three categories: 1) this individual enjoys affluence beyond the average among our prospect base, 2) this individual is average in his or her ability to give, and 3) this individual, for whatever reason, has a limited ability to give.

Once sorted, evaluate the prospects readiness to give. Again, three categories will suffice: 1) This individual has a high readiness to give and has expressed great support for the school system, 2) I have little or no knowledge of this individual's willingness to support, though I know of no problems that would prohibit him or her from making a generous contribution, 3) It is my understanding that this individual has some significant questions about our school's programs or management. Approach with caution.

After broadly separating the prospect base, further refinement of individual askings is needed. You'll want to designate a major gift committee. This should consist of individuals who have given in the range defined as major gifts. This handful of individuals will ultimately be responsible for asking their peers for the gifts in the top giving ranges of the scale of gifts. They must take all of the "1a" and "1b" prospects and decide who could be asked to give in each specific range. The lead gift or next lower giving level must do the same with the lead gift prospects. The remainder of the prospects not picked up for solicitation in

the top two donor categories would then go into general solicitation: mail, phonathon, or other program vehicles.

Developing a scale of gifts

The development of a scale of gifts needs sensitive professional counsel and thoughtful volunteer input. The three
considerations in the development of a scale of gifts are: 1)
the needs of the institution, 2) the constituency's current
giving pattern, and 3) the typical giving pattern of a similar
constituency facing a similar set of problems.

Most prospects will have no previous giving patterns. We
also do not have any typical giving patterns for public
school solicitation of this type. Thus we must look beyond
our current constituency to the wider community to review
the nature and make-up of the charitable support group
available to support the public schools. Each community
that is to be solicited will show a specific giving pattern. For
example, a community that has a constant economic level
throughout the community tends to reflect a flatter scale of
gifts than a community with varying economic levels. Also,
the way a constituency is solicited will determine giving
patterns. For example, an annual fund solicitation seeking
gifts that repeat each year will generate a flatter scale of
gifts than a capital campaign or one-time solicitation focused on a specific project.

Whether one projects a relatively flat giving pattern or
one more significantly skewed toward the larger donor, be
prepared for the fact that approximately 10 percent of your
prospects will need to give in the range of 25 to 30 percent
of the dollars in an annual fund and 80 to 90 perent of a
capital fund campaign. Thus, if you have a prospect base of
1000 donors in a campaign seeking $100,000 for an annual
fund, anticipate that the top 100 donors will need to give in
the range of $30,000. The following chart represents a

broad distribution of gifts needed to raise $100,000 from 1000 prospects:

Percent of donors	Percent of dollars	1,000 donors	$100,000 goal
5%	25%-35%	50 people	25,000-35,000
10%	20%-25%	100 people	20,000-25,000
20%	20%-25%	350 people	20,000-25,000
65%	15%-25%	650 people	15,000-25,000

Testing the validity of the scale of gifts must begin with the solicitation of the board and other leadership of the program. The question is often asked: What percentage of the goal should the board and the leadership it gathers around itself give? No magic percentage of the goal can be appropriately assigned to the board and leadership. However, their pattern of giving must reflect substantial commitment, and demonstrate that this cause numbers among the primary causes they support. Since we are committed to sending people to ask for dollar gifts commensurate with their own giving level, the top donor prospect group must be represented among the board and leadership of the program to insure success.

Many campaigns are lost in soliciting the first ten gifts. If the top prospects do not give the top gifts, a challenging goal cannot be met. It takes too many $25 gifts to make up for one $1,000 gift not received.

The donor base must be reviewed by the volunteer leadership who are going to give and solicit the gifts in that scale. More than one prospect must be identified for each gift needed.

Success will be determined through the effective preparation of volunteers, the sensitive assignment of each asking and solicitor, and the follow through within the solicitation process. Volunteers must be confident that there are people to ask for each of the gifts defined. They must demonstrate their commitment by assuming appropriate roles within the giving pattern needed for success.

Combine a realistic scale of gifts with sensitively presented askings. This will produce success. The institution will have the resources needed for excellence, the solicitor will know that he or she participated in an effective and productive program, and the donor will feel he or she has done his share.

4   Cultivation: Communicating with those who care

Communicating with the school district's constituencies is inevitable. Success will be determined by what you communicate and to whom. Reasons for communicating go way beyond fund raising. First, it is responsible! Administrators of a public trust are expected to provide accurate, non-manipulative presentations of the status of the institution. In the end it is the community that must assume responsibility for its own future. Because public schools are a public trust, ultimately they are the community's responsibility. Those who work for the public in administering school programs have a responsibility to report regularly to the proprietors—the public. It is similar to business, where corporate heads report to the stockholders on quarterly activities and profits.

People make gifts to causes in which they have confidence. Confidence can best be built when individuals have adequate and accurate information available upon which to base their giving decisions. Bad news is only one reason people do not give. If things are going well in a program and the donor is not told, support will diminish rather than grow because of a lack of decision making data.

People naturally want to feel good about themselves and their community. A programed, straightforward presentation of the successes of the district develops informed, confident, and proud donors. Additionally, the more confident the community feels about its schools the more likely it will be to approve a school budget carrying higher taxes.

Publications

The school district can foster confidence in prospective donors by presenting a positive image. Every gesture creates its own image. Publications by the school make statements beyond the ideas represented by the type on the page. Everything from the quality of paper and printing, the style of writing, and the graphic design says that those who work within a particular institution either care for or are indifferent to their job or, more importantly, the individuals they serve.

Every school has a publications program, or at least publishes some information, even if it has no coordinated program. Components of a typical publications program include: school or parents' association news notes, notices of class activities, permission slips, a calendar of activities, programs prepared for special events, student publications, and report cards. Every piece of paper that goes out of the school into a home or community provides an opportunity for the institution to make a statement, clarify a goal, or explain a situation.

Permission slips including a brief rationale for a field trip or extra-curricular activity enable parents to understand better their child's activity and to feel more involved. Notices of class activities prepared on a thermafax machine with low fluid or an overused ditto master can be difficult to read and will irritate parents. Typos and sloppy layout suggest that the activity discussed is not that important, that the individual who prepared the notice is not fully competent, and that "we don't really expect you to read this." On the other hand, people do not necessarily interpret sloppiness and neglect of detail as a reflection of the activities within the classroom. But, for understandable reasons it should be avoided.

People in an increasingly complex society are forced to plan further and further ahead. They're also accustomed to numerous reminders. Monthly or semester calendars of activities are essential if you expect people to participate in programming planned for their benefit. Because of the hectic pace at which people live, a quarterly calendar seldom gives people enough encouragement to participate in an activity. It isn't enough to say, if people cared they'd pay attention.

When a child participates in a concert, play, or an athletic event that has a program, the information must be accurate. Otherwise, you say to parents, "Your child's activity isn't important to us." Student publications that contain numerous errors create an image of weak and ineffective leadership. Report cards that are really the fifth page of an NCR form that renders the initial semester's comments and grades unreadable, deprive the parents of an understanding of the progress of their child. Although it may be efficient for the individual filling out the report card, this efficiency may cost dearly in parent understanding and support.

Ask the following questions about the school's publications: Is the material readable? Is the print face dark and does it contrast with the color paper it's printed on? Is the design attractive? Is the reproduction of pictures good? Are the people in pictures identified? Are pictures captioned so that one can understand them? Are the margins straight? If the publication includes a notice of an event, will it reach the home in adequate time for the family to prepare to attend? Is the style of writing interesting? Is the content accurate? Are answers available to all of the basic questions that the reader needs to make a decision, or take an action? Are the answers easy to understand? Who reads the publications?

The aesthetic effect of the printed page should facilitate the communication of ideas. Often publications can be improved with very little increase in cost. Simply by seeing that machinery used in reproduction works properly will often do a great deal to improve the appearance of the finished product. The time has arrived for outdated duplication equipment to be replaced by electronic word processing systems. The substitution of photo offset duplication for mimeograph or thermafax creates an in-house print capacity and often results in operational savings. Paying for the costs of such improvements can also be seen as a long term investment in the institution. All school districts have allies within the community who would understand such a goal. The corporate community has always been aware of its public image, and it has spent major assets to preserve its good image.

In some instances publications can be improved significantly while decreasing the cost to the institution. Ask a company that has a large public relations or communications department to pre-print a masthead for a student publication, parents' association news notes, or activities calendar. The school can obtain the paper for these publications free of cost if the company is willing to include it as part of its contribution. If the district has an art department that can prepare the mechanical layout for its publications, the cost to the corporation becomes insignificant, particularly compared to the community exposure that it can receive through including a discreet line identifying it.

Another effort that can be jointly undertaken with a corporation is to develop and distribute a well-written and attractively designed annual report highlighting the accomplishments of the district during the past year. This report should be liberally sprinkled with photos and the copy should provide the reader with a comprehensive look at the strengths and goals of the district.

Publications a school should consider are: faculty pictorial directories, alumni "news notes," and a quarterly newsletter for parents and others involved in the school. The primary purpose of these, as in all communications, is to increase confidence and involvement in the institution—two factors that are essential to fund raising.

A school is as strong as its faculty. Traditionally, private schools have wisely spent considerable resources on publicizing their faculty's excellence. It is common for public schools to announce new faculty appointments to the media. Feature articles on outstanding faculty members prepared by the school can also highlight faculty achievements. When these feature stories are photocopied and distributed to parents and alumni, they provide a ringing endorsement of the quality of the school.

Another approach is to develop a faculty yearbook highlighting the achievements and responsibilities of each faculty member. This publication provides an excellent introduction of the faculty to parents and can lead to a closer working relationship. Photographs make faculty more familiar to the parents before faculty-parent conferences are held.

For years private schools have viewed alumni publications as essential. Alumni publications allow the institution to explain its current educational programs and trumpet its strengths to a vital support group. But more importantly an alumni publication contains "alumni news notes." These are more than a record of who is doing what. They provide a vital link between each alumnus and the institution. News notes enable individuals to keep those relationships which were at one time so important, alive and functioning. This facilitates networking and increases the school's importance to the alumni. Moreover, the ultimate measure of the strength of any school program is best demonstrated by the success of its alumni.

A quarterly or monthly newsletter can be produced and funded by consolidating all current "separate page" publications, such as class notices, field trips, press releases. A newsletter profiles the overall strengths of the school's programs. It also serves as a vehicle through which constituents can share problems, provide counsel, and offer support.

Events

As surely as all schools have publications, so do they have events. And likewise, some have a coordinated events program. Commencement, awards assemblies, school plays, and athletic events are all examples. Anything the school does that showcases its students, and therefore its program, provides a chance to inform and cultivate a constituency. The private school views such programming as a series of opportunities; the public school often sees them as necessary evils. These sharply differing perspectives convey two sharply different messages to the public about the school's attitudes toward its students and their families.

These events should be evaluated regularly in light of the following questions. Do the events come off smoothly and professionally? Do guests at the school know upon entering the building where to go and what they are to do? Do the events provide any moments of inspiration to the viewer? Are the programs entertaining and well-paced? Do they appear well-rehearsed?

Making events attractive and meaningful does not have to be expensive. How many parents would not provide refreshments to enhance a concert in which their child is participating?

Spend time preparing invitations. Be certain that they are received in a timely fashion. Today's families are living in a hectic world; therefore, planning is essential if parents are to attend an event that features their child. Bringing parents into the building provides the school with a chance to point out its strengths.

Unless resources are available to hire a paid staff, rely on volunteers. Volunteers are generally available and willing to work if they feel that their job is important and that they are making a significant contribution to their child and the school. Consider setting aside space within the school for volunteers. Many private school parent associations require little more. An attractive meeting room for parent association officers can encourage them to raise their sights as to what they can do for the school. This space could also be the display center for the school's traditions and awards. In the current stainless steel and glass school buildings, history and tradition have nearly been forgotten. Displays of prominent alumni, revered teachers, principals, and others who are part of the district's past promote a sense of longevity and strength as well as preserve a small piece of community history.

All schools have homecoming events of one type or another. Great benefits can be derived from making this an all-community weekend event, which can produce district pride. Make efforts to bring former students' parents back into the school. Let this be a homecoming for the whole community, not just for the high school.

Public relations

Everything that we have talked about so far falls under the broad category of public relations. There is, however, an important dimension of public relations that concerns public schools: media relations. The public's perception of the school district can be molded by a comprehensive media relations program. An effective media relations effort transmits a readily understandable message to the desired audience. To be successful, a program must be comprehensive, consistent, and continuous. A well constructed media relations program should target:

> 1. Strengthening the district's schools by keeping their names before the public in a favorable light.

2. Explaining how all aspects of the public school experience—academic, sports, arts, alumni and parent activities—fit into the school's goals for excellence.

3. Helping to position the local school district as an educational vanguard in the region.

4. Slowing the private school "brain drain" by stimulating interest in what the district's schools have to offer.

5. Supporting fund raising efforts by increasing the school district's recognition by corporations, organizations, and individuals.

6. Helping to increase the morale of faculty, staff, and students.

Being part of a well written feature story, appearing favorably in news columns, serving as a source of educational trend articles, and having the schools of the district discussed on the air are the results of a good media relations program. Media relations may be divided into two segments: print and broadcast.

The print media reaches a cross section of the population through a variety of approaches: the mass appeal of a general newspaper, the editorial page, the individualized attraction of a special section (sports, lifestyle, business), local weeklies, shopper's guides, and business reviews. In addition, professional journals, corporate newsletters, and alumni bulletins can play special roles.

Knowing how to reach the media is the key. Do not look for the media to do your work. It is essential to understand the criteria reporters and editors use in selecting materials to be published or broadcast. Recognize that when the school or its students receive an award an opportunity is created to explain the excellence of the program that attracted that award. Everyone is aware that the press will focus on district affairs when something goes wrong. However, it will also focus on a positive affair if it's newsworthy.

Work with the media and do not expect them to coddle you. Check your stories for accuracy and punctuation. Make sure they are concise and readable. Always provide a contact person and furnish backup material so that a reporter can do an "in depth." Plan your new activities so that they can coincide with the schedules of the news rooms. Get materials to them ahead of their deadline.

View faculty as a community resource. A well managed media relations program will continually connect the media with faculty knowledgeable on specific issues.

Although media relations are essential to fund raising, personal contact provides the greatest public relations opportunity for the school. The bulk of the personal contact is between parent and faculty. Encourage the faculty to communicate, communicate, communicate. The faculty should contact parents not only with problems but with commendations. Provide administrative support to faculty who are willing to follow through.

5 Cultivation: Developing meaningful involvement

Involvement is a subjective word. For some, a significant involvement with an organization consists of a bi-monthly meeting with no intermediate activities. For others weekly participation is the norm.

Section 1—Understanding involvement

Volunteers can be involved in an organization three ways: 1) as a director/policy maker who serves the institution as a member of the board of directors, as a trustee, as a member of an advisory committee or other body that establishes policy and oversees implementation; 2) as a program volunteer; 3) as a contributor of money or personal goods.

Participation occurs on two levels. A level *a* participator is intentional, direct, and active. A level *b* participant is casual, vicarious, and passive.

Everyone passes through four stages on their way from new acquaintance to head of the board.

Stages of involvement

Stage 1	Collects information
Stage 2	Demonstrates concerned interest
Stage 3	Begins personal involvement
Stage 4	Assumes personal responsibility

Stage 1—Informational stage

A person must have an understanding of the goals of the institution. Much of the time, transmission of the goals can be accomplished through an effective public relations and publications program. Begin cultivation by informing people about the institution. Establish programs that enhance the ambience of the institution and strengthen public opinion concerning the cause.

However, cultivation does not conclude when one has built public relations, publications, and event programs that effectively present the institution to its constituencies. Thinking about an organization is involvement at one level. But thinking must lead to activities and resources that will insure future stability. Therefore, develop programming that carries individuals from the informative stage to Stage 4 (assuming personal responsibility).

Stage 2—Demonstration of concerned interest

Many times people are ready to move from Stage 1 to Stage 2 but have no appropriate way to signal the institution of their intention. An effective program of parent seminars on issues surrounding the education of their children, attractively run open houses, introducing parents to faculty and staff, meaningful class reunions, and the opportunity to participate in special funding for projects and programs within the district, provide individuals with an opportunity to signal their intention to grow in their knowledge and understanding of the programs and issues of the district.

The first-time donor would be placed in Stage 2. Although still relatively passive in his or her identification with the cause, the donor is making the statement, "Something needs to be done!"

Stage 3—Beginning of personal involvement

The next step is obviously to identify those who are regularly in attendance at seminars and other events and who are making their first contributions to the institution. After identification, determine who is willing to assume a more constant involvement, such as becoming a program volunteer, or who is interested in making a special project possible through another contribution.

Stage 3 marks the beginning of volunteering. The staff must realize that the volunteers are there first to enhance the program. Once involved, some volunteers persuade others to join them in making an even greater program possible.

Whether it is recruiting program volunteers or soliciting annual fund dollars, the message is always, "Come, put extra meaning in your life through joining with others and making possible something that none of us could do alone." Volunteers and prospects must never lose sight of the vision of a better community achieved through collective work.

Provide meaningful involvement. Remember, new volunteers must be nurtured as an infant is nurtured from childhood to adulthood.

Be certain that volunteers are asked to perform the correct job for them. Ask the volunteers to do something specific that has measurable goals. Every task must be carefully defined and a job description developed identifying: 1) the goals of the task; 2) the procedures involved; 3) the time that it is likely to take; and 4) the duration of time in which you expect the volunteer to assume responsibility.

To prepare an appropriate asking for work or money, do research on prospective volunteers. The following data concerning the prospect must be gathered: historical relationship with the district, participation in other volunteer activities within the community, identification of special interests that are indicated through a review of their total giving and volunteer activity pattern, and special skills that might be employed in meeting specific needs. A composite of the above information should provide clues as to the prospect's special areas of concern and where they might best fit into the fund raising campaign. The composite should point to areas of involvement that would provide special meaning in their lives.

Stage 4—Assuming individual responsibility

The heightened involvement and giving patterns of some individuals simply reflect the degree of personal responsibility that they assume in pursuit of commonly held goals. The level of personal involvement indicated by such giving is something that has been developed very carefully over a significant period of time. One does not automatically move from one stage of involvement to the other. Nor can people be rushed in their development from stage to stage. Seldom do individuals jump stages and perform with the depth of understanding and level of personal commitment that will be necessary to succeed at a higher level.

Often, a by-product of passing time is a quite natural increase in involvement. This will only happen when the current level of involvement provides a meaningful outlet for the volunteer's charitable intentions and serves to fulfill personal goals for a healthier community.

Ultimately, the volunteer must become the leader of others. In many cases, staff can motivate others with great effectiveness; however, once individuals arrive at Stage 4, it is volunteer-to-volunteer communication that is vital. Programming for Stage 4 involves personal contact between those who either are or will be on a first name basis.

Section 2—Involvement opportunities

The first rule in developing involvement opportunities: if you ask for volunteers, you must truly want to employ them. Never view volunteers as a necessary evil leading to opportunities beyond. Such a belief shortchanges both the potential for employing volunteers and the volunteers themselves.

The second rule is that there is room for everyone to have a meaningful role in the maintenance and advancement of the institution. The school district is governed by the community and those who work within the schools work to strengthen the community. One might take lessons here from private schools who have gone a long way in identifying meaningful roles for volunteers within the daily operations and annual management cycle of the institution. Volunteer activity does not succeed unattended. Staff must ensure the effective coordination of volunteer activities and the smooth transition of volunteer leadership.

The ways to involve volunteers in the daily life and management of the school district are as wide and varied as the people involved. The following is a list of broad categories for involvement that will hopefully serve as a springboard for other creative ideas.

Involvement opportunity 1—policymakers

There exists in nearly every community in the nation a school board, elected or appointed, making decisions concerning the policy and operations of the local school district. In many communities, there now also exists a board of trustees of a private foundation established to augment and strengthen the programs already in existence. Both governing bodies have from time to time established commissions, study committees, and advisory groups to strengthen their ability to address a given concern. Carefully balanced, such groups provide a broader base of thoughtful input. This policy making level provides the highest opportunity for volunteer involvement.

Involvement opportunity 2—users

Those who benefit from the work of an institution are often in a unique position to provide counsel to the policy makers and program managers. Direct involvement at both the policy making and management level is common today. It often provides a channel for a quality and level of support not unlike the participatory techniques of some factories and other businesses.

Institutional advancement and strengthening comes when all involved determine that there will be a change. Students from eight to eighty who are involved in the various programs of the public schools have the resources to strengthen both the quality of life within the schools and the strengths of its programs.

Conduct special programming to develop and enhance the students' pride and personal ownership in the daily governance and activities of the district. Students are capable of sitting on specially designed advisory panels that discuss the development of curriculum and the enhancement of student life. Students can often be effective spokespersons for the district and its programs, providing a level of endorsement that is impossible from any other group. Such involvement can also mean the vicarious involvement of parents as they watch the participation of their children.

The development of resources is the task of the whole institution. Students must be sensitized to their potential role in this development. When prospective donors come to an institution, they expect to see proud, active, and engaged students who speak to others with sensitivity and respect.

Involvement opportunity 3—staff and faculty

Those charged with the daily operations of the school can often provide the best presentation of strengths and needs.

Develop programming that involves faculty. Staff and faculty are often best at crystallizing the general need and establishing specific program goals.

The tone of any program is often set by the faculty. When they feel comfortable, challenged, and productively involved, the tone is positive and open. When the faculty feel excluded, manipulated, or misemployed the tone is one of confusion, frustration, and often hostility.

The attitudes of the faculty get transferred to the students and inevitably come up at home. When the transmission is positive, the community responds with significant additional support. Transmission of negatives obviously provides the opposite.

Often a solicitation team of a lead volunteer who is already committed, a faculty member, and a student provides the range of expression, endorsement, and challenge that can prompt significant giving.

Involvement opportunity 4—parents

In many public schools today, principals and other administrators feel successful when they develop a parent organization requiring little or no staff support. However, this attitude often leads to either erratic performance on the part of the volunteer structures or conflict between administrator and volunteer.

Providing effective administrative support produces a parent involvement that exceeds anything accomplished by boosters and parent-teacher organizations, which have in the past raised $2,500 to buy a new computer or scoreboard. Effective staff support can lead the volunteer structure into a more coordinated effort eventually providing far more dollars to the program than the support will cost. Effective staff support will provide for a smooth transition of volunteer leadership.

In many communities, parent involvement is already exemplary. Though it is generally staff endorsed it is seldom staff supported. Parents are often involved as lunchroom monitors, library assistants, teacher aides, special projects coordinators, career day speakers, and assistants in athletics. All such activities provide the opportunity for involvement that can lead people from Stage 2 to Stage 3 and eventually to Stage 4.

Involvement opportunity 5—vendors

It is often inappropriate to ask an individual making his living from a product or service to contribute that product or service to a good cause. It is *always* appropriate to present the bidding and acquisition process so that the vendors are aware they have an opportunity to participate in the development of a stronger community.

With the development of an annual fund inevitably comes the opportunity for vendors to make a cash contribution. If an effective job has been done in cultivating vendors and coordinating their support, their gifts should be larger and more meaningful.

Involvement opportunity 6—alumni

The proof of the product's quality is the district's alumni. Answering the question "Who are they and what are they doing?" provides a composite picture of the quality of the district's program. Alumni have a special vantage point from which to view the district, for they became who they are while growing up within the community.

Involving alumni can offer the district the greatest opportunity for gaining new volunteers. Putting alumni on executive search committees that choose the superintendent, key administrators, key athletic appointments, and department heads, can prompt commitment that eventually translates into dollars.

Athletic booster clubs offer an involvement for parents. They also offer a meaningful way for alumni to maintain contact with the programs of the district and provide significant support. A development of an athletic hall of fame recognizing former athletic heroes will bring the alumni back to the school and in time, if well managed, develop strong alumni support.

In recent years, colleges and universities have begun developing programs that involve alumni in the interviewing process for students seeking admission. The school district can turn this around to assist in the placement of current students in the college of their choice. Not only does this provide meaningful support to individual students, it also provides a link between the school district and key colleges and universities that can be productive to both.

Similarly, involving alumni in career counseling and job placement produces a meaningful connection between the alumni and district programs. Alumni can serve as speakers at career days, and as professional experts in the classrooms. In some situations alumni can employ students as interns in their businesses. These involvements can enhance alumni knowledge and insight of the district. In addition, the alumni as role models can make a significant statement to the students.

Obviously, when setting up an alumni program for the district, make sure alumni are in the driver's seat and that it is their effort that makes the program work.

Give thought to establishing a class agent system similar to what is found in a private school. This system provides the avenue of communication between the district and the membership of that class. Such a structure also enhances the planning and implementation of class reunion activities, and in time it builds a base for solicitation of alumni.

Section 3—Rules for avoiding self-interest meddling

1. Clearly delineate responsibilities.

2. Invest in a program that assures effective administrative support to the volunteer sector. Coordination avoids accidents.

3. Identify and publically affirm healthy involvement. Promote it.

4. Leadership selection is the key to health.

5. Planning—long range and implementation work calendars must be developed.

6. Keep informed of what others are doing.

7. Those in positions of responsibility must see volunteer involvement as a positive thing.

8. Make sure people can freely express their concerns and special interests.

9. Provide everyone with the opportunity to make a positive and real contribution through their own fields of expertise or interests.

6 Solicitation means personal communication

Attitudes are important when soliciting gifts on behalf of any cause. The most productive attitude stems from an understanding that solicitation is but one facet of the relationship between individuals and institutions. To build the best relationship between the two, pay attention to developing each constituent's understanding of the goals the individual and institution hold in common.

Healthy attitudes prompt meaningful gifts

In any fund raising program both institution and individual supporters seek to fulfill their goals with the aid of the other. The institution strives to produce a stronger program that enriches and satisfies the needs of its constituencies. Similarly, individual motivation for contributing towards a stronger public school program is grounded in a vision of a better community. The improvement of a public school program can pave the way for positive change in the community. Consequently, the broad, long-range goals articulated by institutions and individuals often are expressed in lofty terms.

Although this vision may be noble, it is not enough. The solicitor must translate these abstract goals into tangible objectives. The solicitor, therefore, must inform the prospective donors of the school district's goals and opportunities and present them with a blueprint that outlines the role they can play in meeting these goals.

Solicitors also serve prospective donors and themselves. The dictates of common sense, as well as the academic disciplines of psychology and sociology, tell us that giving to others helps one maintain a healthy balance in life.

Individuals affirm their own existence most fully when it is apparent that something they have done has had a positive effect on someone or something else. Properly constructed, the giving situation provides donors with an opportunity to sense their self-worth by understanding the significance of their gift. Never underestimate the importance of the chance for personal fulfillment that a solicitor offers to prospective donors.

A solicitor has a need and a right to feel good. The act of solicitation last year prompted Americans to give billions in quest of stronger and healthier communities. When careful preparation, followed by a sincere and effective presentation, results in an adequate number of donations that provide an extra edge of excellence, the solicitor should feel extremely good. Accepting anything less sells the experience short.

The point of this is to create a "win, win, win" situation. The school district wins by being able to finance additional resources. The community wins by gaining an extra edge of excellence in its public school programs. The donor wins when personal goals are met and individual values are affirmed by accomplishing in concert what could never be done alone. The solicitor wins when his or her efforts bear fruit as the schools graduate more and better prepared alumni.

The role of the solicitor

Soliciting financial support for a cause is a service rather like that of an investment counselor who brings together two parties. One offers an investment opportunity with a potential for profit and the other searches for an appropriate place to channel discretionary income with a potential for growth. The school district is "selling" an opportunity for individuals to invest in a project with potential rewards of better schools. In short, the solicitor is offering a vision of public education excellence to investors who want to "buy in" to an improved school district. The investor's dividend is the feeling of satisfaction from the knowledge that the investment was significant and wisely spent.

Solicitors should bear in mind when calling on old friends that they are making a business call, not a social visit. The purpose is to present the "case" of the school district, and state clearly and concisely the role the prospective donor is asked to play in the fulfillment of the district's stated goals.

The primary role of the solicitor is to ask for money. This role is filled when the solicitor, before embarking on a fund raising program, becomes a donor, giving at a level commensurate with the amount to be solicited from prospects. Differences obviously separate the $10 from the $10,000 gift. Small gifts are likely to come from a donor's income; large gifts are probably a transfer of assets. Although the $10 gift must be balanced against daily living expenses, the larger contribution is weighed against the merits of several urgent charitable causes. Gifts of all sizes are essential to a successful campaign. Large and small gifts should bring to each donor the satisfaction of having participated in something worthwhile that could not have been accomplished individually.

The most efficient way to accomplish a fund raising goal is through a series of personal calls made by solicitors upon individuals, corporations, and foundations within the school district's "family." The solicitors recall for the prospective donor the story of the local school district: its history, tradition, and current activities. Properly executed, the call reaffirms the prospect's relationship to his or her alma mater or the district.

Although statistics can accurately predict how many people will die next year, neither statisticians nor the actuaries of the insurance industry can foretell who will die. Similarly, given a large data base, it is equally possible to calculate the results of a standardized solicitation procedure including the number and size of gifts. However, just as the insurance industry cannot predict who will die, a fund raising projection cannot predict who will give what. The only way to determine that is for each solicitor to tell the school district's story in a positive way, provide a realistic, optimistic asking, and trust each prospective donor to make up his or her own mind.

Mental preparation for solicitation

Mental preparation for donor solicitation is more than half the battle. Solicitors should never approach a prospect assuming that, "This will be hard to sell." The solicitor is not there to "sell" the district. He or she is a vehicle for transmitting the message of the schools' strengths and needs. Although in a well orchestrated solicitation the solicitor is provided with an asking to present to the prospective donor, it is not the solicitor's responsibility to determine the proper gift amount. The job of the solicitor is to answer the prospect's questions and provide data that helps the individual's relationship to the district grow.

A solicitor should be confident in the quality of the district's cause and of the prospect's personal integrity. A solicitor offers prospective donors an opportunity to be a part of a tradition and to fulfill personal and community goals through their gifts. The best approach is to be open, honest, and willing to share your own commitment and enthusiasm. The questions "How much do you need?" and "How much do you need from me?" require answers before the donor is presented with an opportunity to give.

The key is to be personal and simple. The best job is always done by those who know the needs of the public schools, are open to the concerns of the donor, and can discuss both in an articulate and conversational style. Talk with the prospects–not at them. Let donors tell of their relationship with the district. If they are upset, let them ventilate. Never argue, instead indicate that the concern will be passed on to an appropriate staff member for response. Never take sides. Individual feelings should be kept silent. Gossip never helps. Do not play one-upmanship–let the prospect tell the best story.

An individual's gift is a manifestation of a personality as it relates to the community. Do not approach a giving situation with a frivolous or joking attitude because the prospect's response is likely to be the same. The ambience of a solicitation experience, although not solemn, is not silly.

The job of the solicitor

The effective solicitor is a busy person. Therefore, when planning for solicitation, expect time to be crucial. Efficiency of movement is essential in the charitable world; therefore, call the prospect and schedule a time for the visit.

Prepare for the call. First, know the prospect, and have an approach carefully designed before arrival. Who is this person? What are his or her interests? What else does he or she give to? What is the prospect's relationship to the district? The answers to these and other questions indicate what to emphasize to make the donor's gift carry the most meaning. Remember, meaningful gifts are larger than those casually given.

There are four fundamental steps to follow when asking for money: state the case, actively listen to and answer the prospect's questions, provide an opportunity to give, and say thank you.

Who are your solicitors?

The first characteristic to look for when seeking solicitors is commitment to the cause. Solicitation cannot be successful if undertaken out of a sense of duty to anything other than the mission of the district. The depth of passion one feels toward creating a stronger school district will determine the individual's success as a solicitor. Therefore, recruit solicitors among those who form the committed core. The best solicitors in church drives always come from the lay officers and the choir.

Not only must solicitors be committed to the purposes of the foundation, they must know its operations and activities. Those new to the foundation will be at a disadvantage when soliciting. Therefore, draw solicitors from those already active in foundation program areas like grants review. The leadership of the solicitation program may have fund raising as their primary or only involvement. However, most solicitors will be most effective when they can speak of their other program role within the foundation.

The third characteristic of the effective solicitor is his or her attention to detail and follow through. Most unsuccessful solicitations fail because they are never completed or are not completed on time.

Solicitors must be selected by their peers. Other workers know how people are seen in the community. The best solicitor will possess personal and professional integrity.

Ten tips on enlisting the best workers

1. *Never coerce/manipulate.* No one has a right to tell another what he or she should do. The task

of the enlister is to recruit the "best" workers, which by definition means the most willing.

2. *Enlist by example.* The first thing that inspires others to work is work itself. Be prepared to speak of the role you have agreed to play in this effort.

3. *Provide accurate job dimensions/descriptions.* If you ever want the individual to work again, you had better be truthful in what this job will take to complete in terms of time and tasks.

4. *Set the position in perspective.* Use an organizational chart. What needs to be done and how will it get accomplished. Do I have to do everything? Who will help me? Who must I help?

5. *Set the program in perspective.* How important is this program? People will volunteer more freely if they understand how important the campaign is and how it will make a better tomorrow. Personal "buying in" and individual ownership of the future are the only ingredients that will bring success.

6. *Tell the prospect why he or she is important to success.* Why me? Am I the last hope, or the best for the job? What do you see in me that makes me better than others for this task? What do you want me to invest of myself?

7. *Tell of others already enlisted.* Who will I be working with? Is this a "going concern" or this enlister's fantasy?

8. *Tell of the success of the program to date.* As our goals are in part measured in terms of dollars, communicate the solicitation success to date. This will serve as an indicator of the level of commitment others are making and speak to the significance and importance of the project.

9. *Ask in the name of the cause, not as a favor to the enlister.* Then prospect does not even have to like you.

10. *The best enlistment is always volunteer to volunteer.*

Never assume new solicitors, no matter how much experience they have had, do not need training. Many seemingly good volunteers come with bad habits, and most come with some misinformation.

Training is best done in groups. Volunteers are more effective when they feel a part of a team effort. Each training session should include:

1. The opportunity for solicitors to affirm their commitment.

2. Orientation to the cause, the work of the foundation.

3. Teaching the mechanics of solicitation.

4. Presentations and activities, like role playing, designed to set the solicitors at ease.

5. The opportunity to select and review prospects. (Because solicitors are busy people the number of solicitations should be kept to three to seven prospects.)

Stating the Case

A solicitor should be aware of the types of statements that go into the development of the case.

a) *Present where we have come from*

Communicate a sense of history. The largest gifts are contributed when the donor is confident that he or she is building upon a tradition of excellence.

Identifying exemplary and illustrative moments of service provides the most effective re-statement of the history and traditions of the institution. Carefully chosen illustrations that document how individuals are stronger because of their time within the school district serve as a better amplification of tradition than hours of reiteration of facts and figures.

b) Present current strengths

Illustrate school district strengths using statistics and "people stories." School officials should provide an ample list of accomplishments that make up the fabric of the institution. Ideally, the solicitor should provide illustrations that carry special meaning to the prospective donor. Such illustrations only grow out of an understanding of priorities and goals of the prospective donor.

A carefully developed statement can persuade donors to give beyond their tax dollars. In the early years of the foundation, it is unlikely that information will have been accumulated on a broad base of potential donors. Therefore, when on a cold call, the best the solicitor can do is carry with him or her a selection of illustrations that cover the broad spectrum of the institution. The best illustrations are generally stories about people who are different because of the exemplary work of the school district.

c) Present today's needs

Solicitors often wonder if they have a responsibility to tell negative as well as positive stories. The answer begins with the basic statement, "One grows strongest when building upon strength." Of course there are problems, and hopefully this program will help meet a number of them. It is not a lie to tell what the school district is doing well first and springboard from that to current needs.

Needs can be presented in a variety of ways. They can be presented from the negative statement illustrating how the school district is held back because it does not have the funds to accomplish its goals. Or needs may be presented from the perspective of the visionary, who illustrates what can be if funds are raised to achieve the goals. Packaging of the need is very important, for one way provides a negative statement, the other provides a vision.

d) How will we satisfy the need?

A key question in the minds of all prospective donors is, "What is already being done?" The solicitor should have data identifying leadership actions that have already been taken to achieve the overall goal. For that reason, the board of directors of the benefiting institution should be among the first to give and their commitment should serve as a bench mark for others.

Few programs begin on a definite day. While the foundation seeks funds to install a language laboratory, which will facilitate the implementation of a new language program in the middle school curriculum, in all likelihood some work with languages has already been done or the planning wouldn't point to the need of such a facility. Therefore, illustrate the achieved successes in the program that needs further funding. The strongest solicitation is provided when the prospective donor has a sense that he or she is joining a winning team, not plugging a hole in the dike.

e) What do you need from me?

Ultimately, such questions must be translated into an asking (see survey Chapter 4) that will illustrate the precise way the prospective donor will participate in the effort. Whether enlisting volunteers or soliciting dollars, specific requests result in more meaningful commitments. When soliciting money for specific equipment, it might be appropriate to ask the donor to give, for instance, the whole electron microscope.

Listen to and answer the prospect's questions

Prospect questions reveal what is important to that individual and they enable the solicitor to package the asking in a more personal and meaningful way. If most of the questions of the prospect center on the strengths or weaknesses of the science program at the high school the most meaningful gift probably is one which strengthens the high school science program. If the prospective donor has no questions, he generally has no commitment. Questions provide an opportunity for the prospective donor to understand the goals the solicitor is pursuing. Never avoid questions for they provide the solicitor with another opportunity to restate the case.

Provide an opportunity to give—to invest

As stated earlier, it is not the solicitor's responsibility to say what another ought, should, or can do. However, the job of the solicitor is not completed until the prospect is offered a specific role in the fulfillment of the district's goals.

One sentence serves the solicitor best: "It is hoped that you will consider a gift in the range of $. . ." Using such a sentence does not put the prospect on the spot or put the solicitor in a presumptive posture. The dollar asking is but one way of stating the investment opportunity being offered to the prospect. Dollars do provide a description of one way to measure a gift. A more meaningful way is to describe the gift in terms of the lives that will be affected. Stories of lives changed and lives yet to be changed provide one of the most compelling ways of establishing the importance of a gift.

Another way of defining the meaning of a gift is to describe the role the gift will play in meeting the overall goals of the district. Use of a scale of gifts is essential in such a process for it enables the individual to understand their own unique and important role in the completion of the overall project.

The above must be stated in deference to the life goals and overall objectives of the individual donor. When the goals of the solicitor, the institution, and the prospective donor all find a common ground, the greatest gift can be expected.

7   Acknowledging and recognizing giving

One of the most important steps in fund raising is gift acknowledgement and recognition. A gift is an investment on the part of the donor. Growth depends upon donors first making an annual contribution regularly. As with any investment, the quality, quantity, and nature of the return on the investment is central to the decision of the donor to reinvest each year. Gift acknowledgement provides the donor with his or her "return on investment."

Gift acknowledgement

Self-defined *a priori* worth may be all that some volunteers need to feel good about their commitment. For most donors, however, the gift acknowledgement program should be carefully designed and executed. A gift acknowledgement brings the donor closer to the cause. The following goals lead to an effective gift acknowledgement program:

1. Thank the donor.
2. Place the donor within the solution to a problem.
3. Restate the case.
4. Prepare the way for next year's gift.

All four goals may be accomplished with one communication. However, it is often advantageous to distribute the gift acknowledgement process over time and among a number of key leaders. Through such a distribution, donors may relive the "return on investment" and get to know the leadership of the district and the foundation.

Thanking the donor must be done promptly, preferably within 48 hours of receipt of the gift. The initial thank you should include the receipt so the donor can deduct the gift from his or her taxes. Law requires that a receipt be written; hence, enclose a brief letter of thanks with a formal receipt.

Keep in mind that receipting gifts is a legal transaction, and take care to ensure the accuracy of the receipting process. Do not assume that the donor's returned check is the receipt. Because of the legal requirements upon the donor and upon the institution, it is important that a copy of the receipt be retained within the foundation files.

Proper processing of a gift received can also materially support effective gift recognition later in the year. The following gift processing procedures are suggested:

1. Upon receipt of a gift, the gift should be entered in a daily log according to the date received. If no computerized data base is maintained a second daily log should be maintained by the constituency.

2. Determine how the donor wishes that gift used: unrestricted, annual fund, restricted gift to a specific program, or a restricted gift to endowment. Notation of any such gift designation should appear on the gift receipt, for it can have a determining effect on larger donors' tax returns.

3. Prepare receipts in triplicate. The original goes to the donor, one copy goes to the donor's file, and one copy goes to the central file maintained alphabetically by donor's name. Some also maintain a second master file according to receipt number. This avoids lost receipts.

Assuming the day when most institutions will be, if they are not already, employing some kind of data base management system on a computer, the above files should still be maintained as support files should the information be improperly entered into the computer, or lost due to hardware failure. Properly programmed, the computer should generate the daily logs, receipts, fund balances, and constituency donor lists when needed.

Many institutions employ separate gift acknowledgement procedures based upon the size of the gifts. For example, the donor of a smaller gift of under $25 may receive a pre-printed card which is sent with an official receipt. Gifts above that amount may receive an initial thank you letter automatically prepared on word processing hardware as part of the receipting process. All word processed individual letters should be periodically reviewed and updated with current stories and data. That initial thank you letter might be phrased:

> Dear _____,
> On behalf of the _____ School District, the officers and administrators of the _____ Foundation acknowledge your gift of $_____ toward our Annual Fund goal of $_____.
> Commitments and generosity such as you have exhibited multiplied by the many donors who are participating in this worthy cause will ensure success in reaching our dollar goal and the fulfillment of our program goal of a stronger education for all citizens of the community.
> Sincerely,
> Executive Director
> _____ Foundation

Saying thank you is only the first step in gift acknowledgement. Step two seeks to place the donor within the solution made possible due to his or her generosity. Step two may be accomplished at the same time as the initial thanks and acknowledgement, or it may be delayed and executed by a letter drafted over the signature of the person responsible for the program. In either case, information should be supplied to the donor indicating how their money was spent.

The most effective way to achieve this goal is to tell a story of a successful accomplishment that was made possible by the donor's generosity. Relate this portion of the gift acknowledgement process to people rather than programs. Illustrate success by telling of a life that was changed. Confidentiality must be observed; therefore, make the story more archetypal than individual.

A second gift acknowledgement letter might be as follows:

Dear _____,

A couple of weeks ago I was told of your generous gift to the computer program being established in our school. Such a program is vital to the growth and development of individuals who will in time be ready to assume their own appropriate leadership role as our alumni have for many years. Often it is simply overcoming the fear of a technology that will be essential for our young people to work effectively in the face of a changing society.

I will never forget one boy, who we will call Johnny. Johnny was an underachiever in school until he learned to express his ideas on a word processor. Now he is in the computer room two to three days a week after school. I'm not sure if we're developing a computer programmer, a philosopher, a historian, or a sociologist, but whatever is now emerging is due partially to his ability to express himself through the employment of a new technology, which was made available to him in part by your gift.

I hope, Mr. and Mrs. _____, that this letter helps you appreciate the change in young lives that your gifts and gifts such as yours are making possible in the _____ School.

Again, thank you for your continued support. I hope you can stop by soon and see the facility and experience the program support made possible through the work of the _____ Foundation.

Sincerely,
Chairman of the Computer Center

The third step is often most effective when it is separated by some time from the gift itself. Often an interval of six months is allowed to elapse. Then the donor receives from either the district superintendent or from the president of the foundation, a letter that restates the case through an overview of programs in operation because of the success of the campaign. Such a letter might be:

Dear _____,

Six months have passed since your generous contribution of $_____ to the _____ Foundation. A great deal has happened in that interval as you may have noticed from our regular publications. A new computer facility has been purchased and installed within the school building. A new scoreboard has been installed at the high school football field. Seven teachers were awarded stipends of $_____ in recognition of their excellence in teaching as identified by students and fellow teachers. Because of half-tuition grants seventy-five faculty and staff were able to attend special seminars and classes to improve their professional skills. Ms. _____, from _____ University was able to spend six weeks of her sabbatical working on her project of _____ and conducting seminars at the high school for advanced physics students.

Such enrichment programs set our community schools apart as institutions providing excellence in education. All of this would not be possible if it were not for the ongoing support of the community through passage of the school tax assessment, which provides the base of the program, faculty, and facility upon which we build. Together, our community enjoys a richness and diversity of program that would not be possible from the tax base alone.

Again, thank you for your continued support.

Sincerely,

President of the Board of Trustees of the

_____ Foundation

Step four, preparing the prospect for the next solicitation, is most effectively done through the employment of peer volunteer workers such as class agents. Communication from the volunteer workers may include a pre-printed card or a personalized communiqué. Two to three weeks before solicitation a letter to prospective donors might be worded:

Dear _____,

Your last gift to the _____ Foundation helped accomplish a great deal. We now have new needs facing us. This year our goal is $_____.

From (date) to (date), volunteers will be working on our annual phonathon/lead gift solicitation. When you are contacted, I hope you will respond with the same kind of generosity that motivated your gift last year. As you can imagine, inflation is part of the cause for our increase in campaign goal from $_____ in 1985 to $_____ in 1986. More than that, our ambition for a stronger and better community forces us to reach further than ever before. Your support is essential to the success toward which we all strive.

Sincerely,

Class agent for Grade 7

of the _____ School

−or−

Class agent, Class of '59

Gift recognition

Gift recognition is as important as gift acknowledgement. Properly conducted, a program designed to recognize giving to the district's foundation will both encourage next year's gift and provide leadership to those who did not give this year. The annual publication of an honor roll of donors (a listing of all donors by appropriate categories such as constituency groups and giving level) helps individuals establish a pattern of giving, which is vital to an ongoing program. Not only does it establish a pattern of giving, but it enables individuals to identify with their peer group and build an *esprit de corps*. Finally, publishing such a list identifies leadership and enables them to tastefully establish the bench mark for others to follow.

A carefully managed public relations program that chronicles the success of the campaign can do a great deal toward building momentum during the period of solicitation. Regular news releases should be distributed as the campaign passes intermediate goals. The halfway mark in a campaign is often a time to develop such a news release. At the conclusion of the lead gift portion of the campaign, just prior to the general phonathon, or at the conclusion of the board solicitation, announcing the board gift for this year can provide motivation to the broad prospect base. Publishing special large gifts from individuals or organizations also provides an opportunity to increase success.

Most capital campaigns provide naming gift opportunities (the opportunity for an individual, corporation or foundation to completely fund a specific project). Gifts must, of course, be central to the accomplishment of the overall goals established by the foundation. Exercise caution when using naming gift opportunities in an annual fund, for generally the emphasis in the annual fund is upon unrestricted support. In addition, the annual fund goal generally depends on a broader base of individual small gift support, which is unlike a capital campaign where a higher percentage of the goal is borne by a smaller percentage of the donors.

In lieu of naming gifts, establish giving clubs. Such clubs are vehicles for recognizing unrestricted giving within specific dollar ranges. Membership categories serve the same purpose in organizations that enlist members, such as museums, orchestras, etc. It is often easier for solicitors to ask an individual to join a specific donor club rather than to give a specific amount.

Donor clubs also provide a stepladder of giving, and individuals can be encouraged to move from one club to the next as their involvement and commitment to the institution increases. In many instances, donor club members recruit new members for their club each year. Donor clubs should not operate independently.

Building *esprit de corps* among the donor base is essential. People like to feel they are on a winning team. Therefore, develop events, such as donor recognition dinners, that bring together individuals of the same giving category so they may be thanked and "see what company they keep."

SECTION TWO—

Establishing and maintaining a complete development program

8 Designing an effective first program in institutional development

Before setting out on a journey one must first decide where one wants to go. Next, the effective planner surveys programming already in place that will complete the plan. Finally, new programs are designed as needed and the journey begins.

Let's begin by distinguishing between goals and ideals. The district may ascribe to the ideal of having a strong alumni support program. It then must develop a set of realistic goals and program objectives to meet the district's ideal.

Goals rank daily activities in order of priority. They must be stated in concrete terms and be measurable. Responsibility for their accomplishment must be assigned to specific individuals. An essential component of any goal is its deadline for fulfillment. Goals may be divided into long and short range goals.

Long range goals sit on the outside edge of measurability—close to ideals. Fulfillment of long range goals usually takes years or decades. Therefore, long range goals tend to be more general. If an ideal of the district is:

To maintain a strong alumni support program,

long range goals might be:

> To involve alumni in the instructional programs and college placement activities of the district.
>
> To solicit alumni on behalf of a district annual fund which will support innovative programs in the classroom.
>
> To develop a sense of "network" among alumni.

Short range goals divide the long range goals into even more specific and measurable programs. Given the long range goal:

> To develop a sense of "network" among alumni,

supporting short range goals might be:

> To promote alumni-to-alumni contact through hosting three alumni social events this year.
>
> To initiate a communications program, district-to-alumni and alumni-to-alumni.
>
> To identify, locate, and interview three local alumni per graduating class, and recruit one from each class to be class agent.

Short range goals are in turn supported by program objectives. Given the short range goal,

> To identify, locate, and interview three local alumni per graduating class, and recruit one from each class to be class agent,

program objectives might be:

> To ask long-time faculty for suggestions for possible class agents among the teacher's former students.
>
> To host old alumni and identify local alumni.
>
> To prepare job descriptions for volunteers in class agent program.
>
> To identify and recruit individuals from among alumni of upcoming 10th, 25th, and 40th year re-

union class to be members of a "Decade Steering Committee" that will function as a central recruitment committee.

To convene the "Decade Steering Committee." Ask them to rate prospects identified through the reunions, train them in enlistment strategies, and have them pick prospects to enlist.

To enlist a class agent for each five year reunion class. Repeat each year until all classes are filled.

Goal setting—state the mission

Setting realistic and responsible goals is the most critical step in the planning process. A goal set too low robs the district of needed resources. A goal set too high, and not met, robs the volunteer of a feeling of accomplishment. How then does an institution set a goal? View goal setting as a process rather than an event. The first step in that process is gathering data essential for decision making.

The first data needed is a mission statement. The vision and plan of action reflected in the mission statement will more than any other factor determine the success of the program. What does current leadership hope to accomplish? Whose lives will be affected and how? What programs will be strengthened and how? How will the community be changed? Here are two sample mission statements that can be used as guides. The first is for a foundation that operates summer camps and personal growth programs. The second is for a public education foundation.

Mission Statement of the Aloha Foundation

The Aloha Foundation is a non-profit educational institution with the objectives of fostering personal growth, self-reliance, self-confidence, cooperation, and a sense of community in people of all ages, but particularly in young boys and girls.

These objectives are accomplished through a variety of experiences including camping, hiking, athletics, water sports, art, music, crafts, theater, and environmental education. In a warm and caring atmosphere, Aloha's professional staff nurtures the health and well-being of individuals and helps guide them through challenging experiences that enrich their lives.

Mission Statement of the Paterson Education Foundation

To establish The Paterson Foundation, a broad-based, charitable non-profit community organization, whose purpose is to secure resources from individuals, corporations and foundations. The resources will be distributed to support programs for the benefit of the students in the Paterson Public Schools, for which federal, state and local funding has not been available, and which will lead to the overall improvement of the quality of education and an enhancement of community support for public education.

A vision can often be developed through a strategic planning session participated in by the whole volunteer leadership group. Such a session can be conducted in many ways. The following is one outline of such a session:

1. Ask each participant to generate three to five projects, in order of priority, they feel should be accomplished in the next two to five years.

2. List all projects with duplicate listings. Do not identify who suggested which activities.

3. Have the participants group similar projects with no reference to viability.

4. Lead the participants through a discussion of each project group identifying the goal inherent within the activities. Again, avoid discussion of viability.

5. List all goals identified.

6. Discuss each goal as to appropriateness and viability.

7. Develop a priority listing of goals affirmed.

8. Ask staff to write trial mission statement for review at the next meeting.

Goal setting—identify needs and objectives

After affirming a trial mission statement encompassing the goals identified by the volunteers, develop a trial action plan using the projects and objectives identified during goal setting. Such a plan should reflect staff time and direct costs related to each project or objective. This trial plan of action will serve as a "wish list" and should encompass all programs and objectives identified to date.

Having decided where to go, the next step is to determine what resources are needed to get there. Before trying to decide how much money needs to be raised to meet the projected goals, spend time identifying resources already available that could contribute to success. Is there a potential for earned income inherent within any of the programs identified? What could be accomplished by volunteers with few or no dollars? Finally, assuming anything is possible, determine how many new dollars are needed to fulfill the "wish list."

Goal setting—testing the leadership

Previously, only needs have been addressed; however, the question still remains, "How much money can be raised?" The answer begins with the board of trustees and a few other key leaders. Besides the quality of the mission statement the most important factor that determines success is the strength and commitment of the leadership.

Gift receiving begins with leadership assuming its share of the burden. Volunteer effort, as essential as it is, never substitutes for dollars. Leadership should provide both, and it should give both up front. Without such a personal statement, few will follow.

Before anyone can be expected to give a "fair share," a fair share must be defined. Significant dollars are not raised by everyone giving the average. Goals are met by people giving according to their ability to give and their commitment to the goals. To raise $100,000 from 1,000 prospects, do not expect each prospect to give $100. Normally, a few will give a lot and a lot will give a little. The following giving pattern reflects what happens in most successful annual fund programs.

Scale of gifts
Annual fund goal—$100,000.
Anticipating 1,000 donors

% of Donors	# of Donors	Give % of Goal
5	50	25
10	100	25
20	200	25
65	650	25

Within each donor category are subscales. It is unlikely that $100,000 can be raised without some people giving $3,000-$5,000. Whatever the trial goal is, such a scale of gifts is needed to initially assist the leadership team and later each donor in determining their own fair share. If leadership determines that it cannot give its fair share, consider lowering the goal.

The question is often asked, "How much must the leadership give?" No firm answer exists because relative affluence varies from group to group. What can be said is that leadership should assume a greater share than it expects from others. It is not unusual for the leadership to contribute 30 percent of the goal or more.

Goal setting—identify institutional strengths and constituency readiness

Having defined a set of trial goals and having determined that the leadership can spearhead the program in both effort and dollars, the one remaining piece of data essential to effective planning is whether or not there is the community support necessary to accomplish the goals. To assist in making that determination, leadership often commissions an outside consultant to conduct a feasibility/planning study.

A feasibility/planning study tests the readiness of the institution to raise funds. It ascertains the degree to which an institution is perceived by its public to be worthy of support. If worthy, the institution can offer a compelling cause for donations to a clearly defined constituency. The study also measures the current capability of an institution to capitalize on, and test the depth of, the reservoir of trust and goodwill developed over time.

The feasibility/planning study staff gathers data concerning the institution's volunteer support history, potential giving strength of the constituency, and previous giving history. From this data the consultant develops an institutional abstract.

Then, to protect confidentiality and encourage interviewee candor, the consultant interviews individual prospects and gathers subjective evaluations of the district's programs and leadership. Questions include:

1. How does the prospective donor view current leadership—school board? Staff? Foundation leadership?

2. What qualities are ascribed to the programs of the district?

3. What is the current understanding of the needs?

4. How does the prospect feel about the foundation's trial mission statement? Action plan?

5. What significant misunderstandings currently exist within the mind of the prospect?

6. What is the constituency's ability to give?

7. What is the prospect's current readiness to give?

8. Is there sufficient leadership to conduct a program?

The data received forms a second institutional abstract.

Those who participate in the interviews are selected by the volunteer leadership and staff and should provide a representative sampling of those who will support the cause.

Next the consultant merges these divergent and sometimes conflicting data bases into an institutional profile. That profile is then compared with other institutions of a similar nature and size who have conducted successful campaigns. Then, the consultant adds knowledge and experience of the varieties of programming possibilities open to the district and prepares a report on the findings for the volunteer leadership.

Finally, illuminated by the consultant's perception of the general ambience within the institution and the community, trial program and dollar goals are projected. At this point, the program designs should integrate the vision of the volunteer leadership with the strengths and needs of the school district. Through this process, program goals are refined in light of an emerging awareness of what would enable the institution to capitalize on its current strengths and compensate for any current weaknesses.

The conclusion of the feasibility/planning study signals the end of the data gathering phase of program design. At this time the volunteers and staff should know where they are going. They should also have set specific dollar and program goals, know where they enjoy strength, know where they have needs to meet, and be ready to develop specific strategies to get there.

Program design—refining objectives

Fund raising is never a stand alone program. Successful solicitation is always the next to the last step in a much longer process. No matter how worthy the cause, solicitation will fail if cultivation is ignored. After program and dollar goals come into focus, the next stage is defining what must happen to build the best ambience for fund raising.

The results of the feasibility/planning study should provide the direction necessary to establish a positive ambience for solicitation. First list what issues must be addressed prior to asking for money.

1. Are there any serious misunderstandings that must be addressed? Are constituents aware of what the district is involved in?

2. Does the community understand the excellence that is in place?

3. Are parents actively involved in the life of the schools? Do they feel excluded and powerless to influence what happens to their child?

4. Do alumni have any sense of how they could be an active part of the lives of today's students?

5. Does the community feel separated from the district leadership?

6. Do past supporters still feel a part of the district? Do they feel appreciated for their contributions?

7. Do people have an accurate understanding of current needs? Do they see any way they can help meet these needs?

8. Do business leaders understand the connection between the health of the public schools and the health of their own businesses?

Develop a specific list of questions or situations to address. Different programs provide distinctly different opportunities to respond to concerns.

Program design—selecting your initial constituencies

Unless unlimited start up funds are available it will be impossible to adequately support start up programming for all constituencies at once. Therefore, a determination must be made as to where to begin. All districts have the same constituency groups—alumni, parents, friends, corporations, and foundations. The key question is, which constituency or constituency subgroup offers the greatest likelihood of up front involvement and support?

To make that determination, divide each constituency into as many clearly defined subgroups as can be identified. A subgroup is any group within the whole, such as parents associated with a particular building or program, and alumni of a particular class or era. Fill out the following form for each constituency or subgroup identified.

Constituency Identification Form

Constituency: _____ Subgroup: _____

Number in Group: _____ Number with Current Address: _____

Number of Active Volunteers: _____ Number of Donors: _____

Regularly receiving the following communications:

Additional opportunities available for communication:

Involvement opportunities open to group:	# Involved

Possible additional involvement opportunities:

Individuals from group who could be considered possible leaders:

Activities of group in last three years:

Questions or situations of concern that must be addressed:

Be careful not to count prospects twice if they are both a parent and an alumnus. Be equally meticulous about identifying an individual's multiple relationships. A parent who is involved in a special program, who is an alumnus, and who regularly hires students in his or her business has many reasons for supporting the district. Defining parent relationships to the district could be facilitated by asking each homeroom teacher to have his or her students complete a brief questionnaire.

Family Relationship Questionnaire

Student Name: _____ School: _____
Fathers Name: _____ Did he attend school in town? Y N
Mother's Maiden Name: _____ Did she attend school in town? Y N

An individual should be assigned one primary classification. Generally that classification is determined according to how they will be solicited—as a member of the district leadership, as an alumnus, as a parent of XYZ school.

The key to developing a successful program is to build strength upon strength. Take the Constituency Identification Forms and stack them according to level of current involvement. Any groups with a giving history should move to the top of the pile followed by those who have been active volunteers. Put subgroups with no prior activity at the bottom. Then divide the pile according to constituency keeping the most active subgroup on top.

Program design—selecting initial activities

The first principle of selecting activities to begin a program is that the focus must be on the donor and not on the cause. The "correct" program enables the volunteer leaders to share with their peers their vision of a way to together make the community better. People make token gifts to causes. Meaningful gifts are made to other people's causes. Therefore, select activities that bring people into contact with other people—the more personal the contact the larger the gift.

Program decisions must ultimately rest with the volunteers, for they are the principal players and must be comfortable with not only the message but also the forum of the message. Staff is responsible for introducing to the volunteers program alternatives that could be currently managed—but the decision must be the volunteer's.

Finally, remember, the foundation is not looking for activities that will raise money, but rather activities through which volunteers can invest in individual lives.

To begin the selection process take the top three subgroups from each constituency pile and place them, by constituency, across the middle of the desk. Make a list of the seven steps in donor-centered fund raising (the survey chapter titles) and place it at the top of the desk. Fund raising is not difficult if the steps are followed. To skip one step or to rush will diminish the chances for success. Now identify where each subgroup is in the process and assign them a number that corresponds to where they are.

Next bring back to the desk the list of questions and situations you identified earlier that must be addressed to create the most conducive ambience for solicitation. Are the questions all listed on one or more Constituency Identification Forms? If not, add the questions to the appropriate forms.

Bring back to the desk the action plan approved in the goal setting process. The best vehicle for fund raising is often the program made possible by a successful drive, for it is the ultimate statement of the vision. At the very least, the program carried out among the students provides the best backdrop for fund raising.

When reviewing the partial list of program alternatives chart, keep in mind the maturity level of the constituency and any pertinent questions. Furthermore, develop specific objectives for each constituency that will persuade them to become donors.

Activity / Program goals

Activity	Expand/cultivate broad base	Gain exposure in community	Gain exposure among a specific constituency	Provide for solicitation of large donors	Increase an average gift size	Provide forum for presenting success
Recognition dinners	X	X				X
Phonathon	X		X			X
Lead gifts/donor club program			X	X	X	X
Direct mail campaign	X	X	X			X
Alumni magazine	X		X			X
Parent publication	X		X			X
Alumni activities	X	X	X	X	X	X
Class agent program	X		X	X	X	X
Foundation or school board annual report	X	X	X			X
Donor recognition program/publications			X	X	X	X
Publish community newsletter	X	X	X		X	

Partial list of program alternatives

Finally, take the specific objectives, and the rationale for each, to the volunteer leadership. Then, together select specific activities and instruct staff to develop a cost-benefit analysis. Be very cautious of taking on too much the first year. It is always better to do a few tasks well than to do many tasks half way.

Program design—some words of caution

Most campaigns are won or lost in the design stage. Do not rush the process. Large capital campaigns are often two to three years in planning and design. In fact, actual designing time takes only days. The remaining time is spent in assuring that the volunteers "own" the program before kick off. By the beginning of implementation the volunteers must believe that the objectives are essential and that the goals are vital. And, finally, the volunteers must have faith that it is possible. Be prepared for the initial design phase to take at least six months.

The design phase deliberately includes the solicitation of top leadership. This step must not be avoided or postponed for it tests the validity of the design. If leadership is not willing to provide support at the level required for success, assume there is a fatal flaw in the design.

In selecting activities do not allow, by omission or commission, one constituency group to dominate the others. All have a strategic role to play and each has a unique potential to fulfill.

Recognizing that 80 percent of all dollars given to charity is contributed by individuals, initial programs should expose a broad base to the work of the foundation. Likewise, programming should recognize the individual donor's gift rather than volunteer effort. I repeat again, effort never substitutes for cash. Although both are vital to success, if only one is available, make it cash.

Try to secure a large challenge gift to stimulate giving in the early period of the foundation's development. Such a gift provides both endorsement and motivation to the prospective donor.

All activities selected should provide the donor the opportunity to knowingly make a contribution rather than a purchase. Rather than selling tickets to a play, paid for in part out of foundation resources, give the tickets as a thank you for a gift. Raffles, benefits, casino nights, and other activities can raise money. However, these events seldom build a loyal support base of individuals who feel invested in the future of the school district.

Events generally require a great deal of volunteer energy. Such contributions of energy and creativity often become the prospect's gift, which represents spendable income far below the giving potential of the leadership alone. Twenty to thirty hours of volunteer labor invested in direct solicitation will always net greater returns than the same time invested in making items for a bazaar.

9　Evaluation/design/planning— one process

Evaluation, design, and planning should be viewed as one process, "strategic planning," encompassing three tasks. The tasks share a common goal—to develop a stronger program for the future. To achieve the best results each task should be completed in a specific sequence and should employ interrelated procedures and common data.

Strategic planning often fails because of lack of specific detail concerning past activities. There are specific data bases for operating procedures, costs, benefits, staff, equipment, space and budget all relating to program goals. Develop these data bases early in the strategic planning process. In an ongoing program, much of the data for strategic planning should come out of regularly conducted interim post-activity evaluations.

Develop data in small detail. To plan in months or seasons and then face the need to implement in terms of days can cause ferocious crunch times. This would be especially true at the support staff level. When this happens the result is a costly, under productive office that is a frustrating place to work.

Effective evaluation takes commitment and a considerable investment of time and creativity. Because development professionals and volunteers are busy dealing with a full portfolio of current issues and problems, program review and the development of long range plans can seem unaffordable or unattainable. Because of scheduling realities and reflection time, anticipate the process to take at least six months.

Why strategic planning?

The long range benefits of interim and summary strategic planning sessions are best illustrated by the statement, "You better take time to look where you are going or you might get to where you are headed." Quality strategic planning forces the intrusion of reality. It also provides the mid-course corrections essential to implementing effective programs that fulfill long and short range goals.

The short range benefits include a more pleasant work environment and generally more productive workers. The development of realistic work calendars forces the planning necessary to level out work loads, define responsible individual work portfolios, plan for the acquisition of appropriate hardware, and avoid falling into management by crisis.

The strategic planning process: evaluation/design/planning

Evaluation—Step I. Identify today's needs and strengths—data gathering.

Objective I-A. Begin by identifying the specific goals approved by the board of trustees development committee. Which are met or not met at the time of this evaluation? Strategic planning is a process best initiated in a secure and impartial ambience. The person best suited to evaluate the program that failed is the individual around whom it collapsed. However, for obvious reasons that same person may be the most reluctant to participate in such an evaluation. Be sure that the participants are comfortable and come into the sessions feeling secure.

The best evaluations consider that no program is ever a total failure or a complete success. When cataloging the success in meeting agreed upon objectives, work to divide each objective into its principle tasks, and evaluate the parts as well as the whole. Besides getting the best results such an approach enables the manager with the troubled program to maintain a sense of worth.

It is out of objectives that programs are born. Successful programs generally mean objectives have been met.

Objective I-B. Identify working programs. Another way to eliminate defensiveness during the evaluation process is to collect information concerning each program or task. The facts below develop a clear picture of the level of achievement as measured against the goals established during the previous year's planning process.

1. Number of potential participants.
2. Number of actual participants.
3. Quantified results—dollars raised, people talked to, expressions of support/problems.
4. Volunteer participation/support.

"Working" is a relative term, for all evaluations must be mindful of long term and short term goals. These considerations increase the potential of avoiding a glib review and another potentially limiting situation: institutional entrenchment. A program may be failing to meet short term objectives but at the same time be making progress toward the fulfillment of long range goals, and vice versa.

"Working" is relative because a program cannot be judged as "working" only on what it accomplished. Its effect must be looked at in comparison to its cost. Some good ideas are simply too costly in dollars or staff to use when judged in the light of the benefits to the long range goals of the foundation.

Evaluate programs in terms of their peripheral impact. Often an activity is initiated to meet a specific need that no longer exists, and then the activity takes on a life of its own. This is fine, if that activity has also grown and now fulfills other needs of the institution.

In the end, all programs will have areas where either costs can be lowered, or production increased.

Objective I-C. Identify ways to strengthen programs. Five basic questions to be concerned with:

1. How to accomplish as much as last year with less staff?

2. How to accomplish as much as last year more cost effectively?

3. How to accomplish more than last year?

4. How much will the "more" cost in staff, budget, and volunteer activity?

5. How much to expect from the "more?"

Approach this task in strategic planning mentally unencumbered by staff or budget restraints. Even if increases in both are not possible, the possibility to reallocate resources remains. Free the staff and volunteer leadership to project what *could* be in their program areas with minimal consideration to what *is.*

Next, ask that all department heads and program managers prepare a 95 percent budget—a program budget that employs only 95 percent of last year's resources. List what can be accomplished with that 95 percent budget.

Finally, ask departments to generate a list of programs to add if the resources are available. This list should be ordered according to the priority of implementation. Each item on the list should be supported by a proposal outlining operations with cost and benefits projected specifically.

Objective I-D. Identify the specific resources available to serve the program.

Resource 1. *Staff:* The greatest asset in any office centers on the skills of the staff. Future development of those skills will greatly depend upon regular and thoughtful re-identification and reevaluation of each individual's skills. A valued staff member deserves such a review yearly.

Use this data to redefine the portfolios of the staff to more adequately distribute work load in relation to the skills and interests of the staff.

Such an analysis can also point to staffing structure deficiencies caused by the lack of a specific skill or body of information. Further analysis can help determine if such a skill can be assigned "for development" to a staff person, or if it would be better to hire a specialist from outside for the duration of the specific project.

Resource 2. *Equipment:* Equipment ranks a close second to volunteers in amount of support and frustration provided to the development staff. Both are vital to the success of most programs. Therefore, maintain a log of equipment, its replacement and maintenance costs, its intended use, its utility, and the equipment needs of the office with value estimates.

Resource 3. *Institutional calendar:* The school year itself is a great asset. It already has scheduled celebrations and exhibitions. Opening those events to the general public or a few special guests can provide an excellent opportunity for the cultivation of donor prospects. Such "piggy-backing" also keeps costs in line. Review the school calendar for such opportunities.

Resource 4. *Volunteers:* Volunteers also need the benefit of participating in a program and task evaluation. They too need the opportunity to grow with their job.

Evaluation—Step II. Estimate real potential.

Objective II-A. Conduct staff time study. Develop as much detail concerning the time it takes to do certain basic functions, such as recruit a volunteer, complete a mailing, prepare a publication.

Place staff costs on a grid that projects the staff costs based on the time it takes to complete the component parts of a program. This builds a unit price concept into evaluating potential.

Objective II-B. Conduct Feasibility Study. How much are our volunteers willing to give in dollars and in energy? How do they view the projects under consideration? How do they view the leadership of the foundation and of the district?

Objective II-C. Identify how to further develop potential through program/equipment/staff/budget/calendar changes. Everyone participating in the strategic planning process should have the data to draw some realistic conclusions that will serve as the base for next year's program.

Design—Step III. Developing "trial" program.

Objective III-A. List the coming year's board-approved needs and goals. How will the development office be judged next year at this time? The answers to this question must consider all of the above steps and yet not be entirely conditioned by them. Often challenge can inspire all to do more than they thought they could. We will never do more than we feel is necessary to do the job. Conversely, with proper planning and organization, we can accomplish great things.

Through a process that arrives at consensus among staff and volunteer, and by using the data developed in the feasibility study it would be prudent to establish trial goals around which the development of programs must revolve.

What is needed to positively influence the school district? How does that translate into dollars? How does that translate into programs?

Objective III-B. Identify the field of program components that would meet the foundation's needs, and fulfill its goals. Given the foundation's track record at implementing specific programs, which program components would likely meet the goals listed above?

Objective III-C. Identify the optimum program sequence and calendar. Most programs have optimum times for implementation. Individual program calendars must run smoothly alongside each other.

Operating again on the concept that one seldom gets more than one requests, identify the optimum:

1. sequence of implementation for each task within each program.

2. calendar for completion of each task and program.

Design—Step IV. Project costs associated with implementing trial program design.

Objective IV-A. Identify the number of staff work days needed to complete each task and program. Employing the "staff unit cost accounting grid" developed in Step II, assign a staff cost (time) for each task outlined in the trial program developed in Step III.

Objective IV-B. Identify equipment needed to complete tasks. Employing the equipment utility statistics developed in Step I-D-2, define the equipment needs associated with the effective completion of each task and program.

Objective IV-C. Identify the costs of implementing each task and program.

Planning—Step V. Integrate the results of Steps II, III, & IV.

Objective V-A. Refine "trial" program to meet real work calendar. Now, go back to the volunteers who established the goals and review the projected cost of achieving those goals. In most instances, the desired number of staff exceeds the number actually available. The volunteers must decide what they can do without in terms of staff support.

Reflect any program cutbacks in the goals established for the coming year. It would be unfortunate if volunteers felt failure simply because someone overestimated what could be accomplished. Ensure that staff loads are properly balanced, reflect individual strengths, and require a reasonable work schedule to meet the established performance goals.

Objective V-B. Develop a budget reflecting real program and staff costs. It is likely that enough money will not be available to fund that ideal program. Again, volunteers must decide what to keep and what to delete.

Planning—Step VI. Plot essential support needs.

Objective VI-A. Develop volunteer job descriptions and work calendars.
Objective VI-B. Review and refine staff job descriptions.
Objective VI-C. Develop weekly "tickler files" of project tasks.

STRATEGIC PLANNING CASE STUDY THE ALBANY ACADEMY, ALBANY, NEW YORK

The following pages contain a distillation of the memos and paper work chronicling the strategic planning process of the volunteers and staff as they charted the course for the program following a successful $3,000,000 capital campaign. The segue into a more normal mode of operating was complicated by the fact that before the completion of the capital campaign the office portfolio had already been expanded (with too little planning) to include all publications, public relations and parent relations, as well as maintaining their usual portfolio of alumni relations and fund raising.

The strategic planning process was initiated with the

staff running a four month time study of the tasks of the office. Daily logs were kept detailing just how much time went into each task and program. The following is a representative sample of the results of that study.

Representative task time costs

Program/Tasks	Task Hours	Program Days
Major Committee or Board Meeting		
Update Financial Reports	4	
Update Volunteer Activity Reports	2	
Prepare Committee Hand Outs	2	
Attend Meeting	3	
Prepare and Distribute Minutes	5	
Total Per Meeting		2
One-Two Day Advisory Committee Work Session		
Invitation and Informational Mailings	16	
Preparation of Amenities	12	
Attend Work Sessions	12	
Prepare and Distribute Follow Up Mailings	8	
Total Per Session		6
Gift Accounting and Acknowledgement—		
1,200-1,500 Gifts		100
Write, Publish, Mail 16-20 Page Alumni Magazine		30
Write, Publish, Mail 4 Page Newsletter		4
Write, Publish, Mail 20 Page Annual Report		45

After many hours of discussions between staff and volunteers the following set of goals was written and approved by the Development Committee of the Board of Trustees.

Introduction

The Albany Academy is in the midst of the most significant expansion in institutional advancement programming in the past 5½ years—including the Capital Campaign. One major factor that sets this change apart from a change like the introduction of a capital campaign rests in the permanence of the change. Any special campaign is temporary by definition. However in this instance, to begin the changes being considered means, in many ways, "no turning back."

An expanded base of support has been rediscovered as a result of the Capital Campaign. Much of that new base is as yet untried. Some programming has been started only to discover that with each step forward there is uncovered a new program need to be met before we can realize the new potential.

In such a situation it is important that all parties, staff and volunteer alike, understand and agree with the program goals being established. It is equally important that there is agreement on the procedures to be employed when evaluating each new program and that realistic bench marks of achievement be identified before we begin.

The following paragraphs and outlines are intended to provide trial goals for consideration of the Board's Development Committee. It is hoped they might serve as another step in the development of a realistic long range plan for institutional advancement.

Note as you read goals are in italic and objectives are in regular face. Each program has rationale for the goals presented in narrative form preceding each outline.

Program I: Redesign of the Board's Development Committee

Leadership provides the key to success. The success of the current Capital Campaign can, to a great extent, be attributed to the quality and the constancy of the leadership that has been meeting almost monthly since early April, 1983. The volunteers charged with the ongoing direction and supervision of the program have provided a steady hand and ready support to ensure its success.

To a great extent the whole fund raising and constituency relations effort of the school during the past 2½ years received its focus from the Capital Campaign Cabinet. It provided a focused program, owned by the volunteers, that will be listed over the years among the handful of efforts that have truly changed and strengthened the school for all times!

Thus the *first goal* of this Board's Development Committee reorganization is to *ensure that the clarity of focus that has characterized the program in the past 2½ years is not lost.* That will be no mean task as change always causes confusion before it generates new strength.

Any effort to engage a broader range of alumni and parents in new programs means [second goal] special attention must be paid to the *orientation of the newly enlisted*—a group who will bring fresh ideas and sometimes an impatience with the time careful implementation [keyed to new volunteer ownership] takes.

The Albany Academy has carefully developed for the last five years a program that is unusually invested in the hands of the volunteer. That particular balance has proven to be cost effective, unusually successful, and has provided the pivotal program concept behind the accomplishments achieved to date. Therefore, the *third goal* becomes *maintaining the unique balance of volunteer/staff responsibilities that has characterized past success.* The newly drawn Development Committee must approach its task with the same diligence and sense of ownership as that displayed by the retiring Capital Campaign Cabinet.

A constituency responds to an institution's needs to the degree that it presents a clear vision of a stronger future or a job better done. The *fourth and most important goal* of a newly constituted Development Committee will be *the articulate presentation of the ongoing needs of an Academy of true excellence.*

Redesign of the Board's Development Committee.

A. *Ensure that the clarity of focus that has characterized the program in the past 2½ years is not lost.*

1. Serve as a clearinghouse for all proposed expansions of the school's programs.
2. Provide supervision of the implementation of the program.
3. Conduct intermediate reviews of goals and objectives.

B. *Orient the newly enlisted.*

1. Develop realistic job descriptions for all volunteer positions.
2. Develop action calendars for each program area.
3. Assume an active role in the support of other volunteers.

C. *Maintain the unique balance of volunteer/staff responsibilities that has characterized past success.*

1. Expand the working membership of the development committee to provide leadership for all major program areas.
2. Provide supervision of volunteers to ensure their active participation.
3. Assume responsibility of enlistment of necessary volunteer workers.

D. *Ensure the articulate presentation of the ongoing need of the institution through a careful presentation of the vision of what is and what can be.*

Program II: More effective and increased communications

Historically the Academy led the way among secondary schools in the publication of an alumni magazine. However, soon we were not alone and lately the best have been sur-passing us.

In the past five years the publications program has out of necessity been run as an "add on" to someone's already overcrowded portfolio. At the same time, stringent produc-tion budgets have meant that paying for adequate photog-raphy and design support has been impossible.

This year for the first time we have had the services of an individual whose first responsibility was that publication. The investment paid off. The "print mechanicals" of the coming issue of the *Quarterly* promise a magazine that will provide a yardstick for the future.

The Academy has gone a long way toward fulfilling the *first goal—improving the technical quality of publications—*and will go further in the next fiscal year as the publications budget for design and print has also been increased.

Effective communication in a school like the Academy is a multi-directional effort. The *school* seeks to express its strengths and needs. The *alumni* seek to keep in touch with each other and the school. The *parents* need to know what is going on in the lives of their children. The *boards, administration, faculty* and others responsible for policy making and program implementation need to provide a regular and articulate accounting of their activities to the constituencies. And, the *students* need appropriate chan-nels of expression through which they can test their grow-ing psyches and intellects. The *second goal* of an improved communications program must be *to balance the needs of each constituency in one coordinated effort encompassing publications, events, and utility mailings.*

Access to information is essential to the long term health of a community. The Albany Academy can be proud of re-cent efforts at candor in expressing its strengths and needs. Data has been regularly available to any serious query. Thus, the *third goal* of an enhanced publications program might be stated—*maintain the ready access to informa-*

tion and the clarity of presentation of pertinent issues that has characterized recent years.

One institutional characteristic common to schools like the Academy is the sense of camaraderie among its "family." In the strongest of institutions this feeling is so pervasive that the school's termed "exclusive." Such *esprit de corps* is certainly an asset to any school and must be nurtured. Every event must be run with that goal prominent in the planning and execution. Each publication must be written, edited, and designed so that readers are aware they are a part of a tradition and a network of people that spans time and geography. Therefore, the *fourth goal* could be simply stated—*hold the family together.* Make each communication as personal as possible. Make them more frequent. And always seek to facilitate communication between constituents.

More effective and increased communications

A. Improve the technical quality of all publications.

1. Provide appropriate staff to support the technical preparation of all publications.
2. Insist that all print materials pass through, for review, one central clearing point about school image and consistency of use of logo.
3. Budget more generously to ensure quality of final product.

B. Balance each constituency's needs within one coordinated effort encompassing publications, events, utility mailings, and public relations.

1. Develop a staff position to work beside the publications/public relations manager to ensure an integrated program at the operational level.
2. Develop realistic job description for each publication and event.
3. Develop a realistic production schedule for both.

C. *Maintain the ready access to information and the clarity of presentation of pertinent issues that has characterized recent years.*

D. *Hold the family together.*

1. Develop more personal communication.
2. Communicate more frequently.
3. Develop mechanisms that will facilitate more intraconstituency communication in the form of *Quarterly* class notes, regional mailings, and intraclass communications.

Program III: Expand alumni program

As with the *Alumni Quarterly*, the Academy pioneered the development of an alumni association among secondary schools. The investment in that program contributed, more than any other single factor, to the success we have seen to date in the growth of the Annual Fund and the Capital Campaign. The Albany Academy has one of the most loyal alumni bodies.

In the early days most alumni settled within an easy commute to the campus. Therefore, programming tended to concentrate on events held on the campus scheduled with little or no hope that many from outside a fifty-mile radius would be attending. There was little or no need to publish an alumni directory—the phone book served as well.

More recently some attention has been given to those outside the area and one can see the first regional programs being held in New York, Boston, and Washington. However the emphasis still remains local.

Because of that local emphasis, those outside the capitol district have been allowed to drift away. There is ample evidence of their continued affection and almost "a priori" loyalty. However, affection and loyalty must be exercised to be meaningful, but occasionally receiving an *Alumni Quarterly* does not provide sufficient exercise. People must communicate to feel a part of a family. Therefore, the *first goal* of an expanded alumni program is to *strengthen the fabric of the Academy's family by implementing constituency-to-constituency contacts.*

Communication is an essential first step in the development of a first rate alumni program. However, it is involvement that leads to ownership, and ownership that leads to a sense of responsibility. Thus, the *second goal* is to *develop opportunities for meaningful involvement in the school beyond giving dollars.*

The Albany Academy Annual Fund really found its genesis in the Alumni Loyalty Fund. Responsibility for its operation was later assumed by the school and today with all segments of the family participating it forms the backbone of all of the school's fund raising.

However, alumni participation has fallen, and is a far cry from the recorded high. Therefore, the *third goal* of an expanded alumni program is to *increase alumni participation in the Annual Fund and related Special Gifts*

Expand alumni program

A. Strengthen the fabric of the Academy's family by implementing constituency-to-constituency contacts.

1. Improve the quantity of class notes in the *Alumni Quarterly.*
2. Publish an alumni directory.
3. Institute an ongoing program of research on alumni.
4. Strengthen the *esprit de corps* through more active support of reunion class activities.
   a. Develop class secretaries program.
5. Strengthen alumni programming outside the capitol district.
   a. Provide support for more regional mailings.
   b. Provide support for more regional activities.

B. *Develop opportunities for meaningful involvement in the school beyond giving dollars.*

    1. Social.
    2. Activities in support of programs such as alumni college admissions, career counseling, and career related internships.
    3. Involvement in the governance of the school.

C. *Increase alumni participation in the Annual Fund and Special Gifts Committee.*

    1. Re-build alumni class agent system.
    2. Increase personalization of appeal.

Program IV: Expand parent participation in Annual Fund and Special Gifts Committee

Parental activity on behalf of the school is nothing new. Parent contributions in the form of direct service to program, product, in-kind gifts, and gifts of special equipment and program support are legion.

The parent associations each year host activities and events that do a great deal toward building that sense of family so essential to a country day school. This year for the first time the Development Office has assumed responsibility for the coordination of all those events. The results have been exceptional. Thus, the *first goal* of an expanding parent support program is to *maintain current level of support and coordination of non-fund raising activities of the parent associations.*

People who care as much as Academy parents usually do what they are asked. The obvious explanation as to why our parents do not support the Annual Fund as parents in our sister institutions do is that they have not been asked. The *second goal* of an expanded parent program is to *orient parents to the need for direct annual giving to the school.*

The *third goal* is involving parents more deeply in the Annual Fund with the anticipation that such involvement will *strengthen parent ownership in the fund.*

It has been determined through preliminary research, and on the advice of friends of the school who have knowledge of our parents, that individuals have the means to make substantial gifts out of the ordinary for an annual fund. Therefore, the *fourth goal* for this program is to *strengthen parent ownership in the process designed to solicit special gifts* for the school.

Expand parent participation in annual fund and special gifts

A. *Maintain current level of support and coordination of non-fund raising activities of the parent associations.*

B. *Orient parents to the need for direct giving to the school.*

    1. Headmaster and Board's Development Committee host orientation events for key leadership prospects.

    2. Seek challenge gift to stimulate parent participation.

C. *Strengthen parent ownership in the Annual Fund.*

    1. Increase parent participation in the Development Committee.

    2. Enlist a parent co-chair for the Annual Fund.

    3. Develop parent class agent system to solicit lead gifts to the Annual Fund.

    4. Enlist parents for the new positions who are not heavily involved in current parent programming.

D. *Strengthen parent ownership in the process designed to solicit special gifts.*

    1. Enlist parents to serve on the Special Gifts Committee.

2. Headmaster and parent members of the Special Gifts Committee coordinate specific cultivation program for key special gift prospects.
3. Provide more support and coordination to parent Senior Gift Program.

Program V: Increase giving to the school

There are really only two fundamental organizational approaches to fund raising—individual and broad base. Both must be in place and in balance to achieve maximum results. Each follow the same basic steps but employ different procedures. The common steps are:

1. Identification   4. Involving
2. Evaluation   5. Soliciting
3. Informing   6. Thanking

In broadest terms, the procedures vary along a continuum according to the degree of personalization involved:

Personalized	Generalized
Individual	Broad Base

The largest gifts are produced through a more personalized solicitation to individuals who care by individuals who have already given.

In the past four years the program emphasis has been placed on initiating activities that would eventually support a major gift effort. This focus began in the fall of 1982 when a renewed emphasis on lead gift activity was built into the Annual Fund. At the same time the Board began looking at its own level of giving and ultimately significantly increased its activity and support. The most recent large and successful program designed to increase the base of support was the Herzog Challenge of 1979-80.

The large gift solicitation will soon cease if the broad base programs do not continually turn up new prospects. Thus, the *first goal* is to *increase ownership and participation in the Annual Fund.*

Closure and beginning are both essential to a successful effort. The *second goal* of the new focus in fund raising must be to define the end and *complete the current Capital Campaign* in such a way that all have had a chance to participate.

One goal of a capital campaign is to produce a group of individuals that have been brought closer to the school, but are not ready to make a gift commensurate with their ability to give. Such individuals must not be allowed to recede into the woodwork again. To guard against that [*goal three*] every effort should be made to *convert the Major Gift Committee into a standing Special Gift Committee.*

Increase giving to the school

A. Increase ownership and participation in the Annual Fund.

    1. Strengthen lead gift program.
       a. Involve more local alumni and parents.
       b. Begin satellite lead gift solicitation through regional coordinators.
    2. Initiate class agent program among alumni and parents to concentrate on the percentage of participation.
    3. Increase personalization of appeal.
    4. Expand the phonothons for alumni.

B. Complete current Capital Campaign.

    1. Conduct, over the next five years, a program run through the class agent structure and among the reunion classes seeking 100 percent participation at any level in the Capital Campaign.
    2. Conclude major gift solicitations still outstanding.

C. Convert current Major Gifts Committee into a standing Special Gifts Committee.

1. Seek two members of current committee to become members of new committee to provide continuity.
2. Recruit new members among the major donors from the following groups:
   a. Local alumni.
   b. Non-local alumni.
   c. Parents.
3. Establish a Planned Giving Program.

After adopting the goals listed above, the staff projected the time and dollars that would be required to address the goals. The projections, arranged by program area, were:

Summary of Ideal Program Projections

Please note: Total Days and Total Dollars do not include External Relations

Total Days (Alumni Activities)	373.50
Total Days (Development)	613.75
Total Days (Miscellaneous)	108
	1,905.25
	219.05 (20% interruption time)
	1,314.30
Total Dollars (Alumni)	31,010.00 + 8,000 (Archives)
Total Dollars (Development)	24,375.00
Total Dollars (Miscellaneous)	16,500.00
	$71,885.00
	8,000.00
	$79,885.00

The school budgeted only $66,000 in program dollars and slightly more than 1000 work days. This is what they came up with:

Activity: Communications

Alumni Quarterly (3 issues)	70.5 days	$10,500
Annual Report	35　"	4,500
Parents Newsletter (2 issues) (typesetting, design and layout)	15　"	800

Leadership Newsletter (3 issues)	27 "	1,200
T.L.C. (5 issues)	6 "	125
Planned Giving Mailing (2)	12 "	50
General Pre-Phonathon Mailing	4 "	500
Pre-Lead Gift Mailing (From Chairman)	10 "	50
Gift Recording and Thanks	190 "	
*Regional Mailings (10)	25 "	250
*Class Secretary/Class Agent Prog. (Reunion Classes Only)	30 "	2,500
*Alumni Directory (Research Only)	25 "	250
*NAC (2 meetings)	16 "	3,000
Gallery Openings (4)	10 "	Arts Budget
	475.5 days	$23,725

Activity: Events

Cum Laude	13 days	$ 6,000*
*Regionals (3)	20 (18) "	4,000
Major Donor Dinner	4 "	800
Phonathons (Local only)	20 (12) "	5,000
Mini-Phonathons (4)	16 "	200
Parent Orientation Event (4)	16 "	1,000
New Faculty Reception	3.5 "	250
Homecoming	7 "	500
Mid-Winter Dinner	7 "	900
Guidon	7 "	100
*Competitive Day	10 "	2,000
	140.5 days	$15,750

*Dollars not included in total.

Activity: Development/Solicitation

Lead Gift Program	30 days	150
Senior Parent Gift Program	20 "	250
Parent Class Agent Program (Upper School only)	12.5 "	250
Alumni Class Agent Mailings (2)	32 "	1,000
Regional Lead Gift Program (2 Regions only)	17 "	1,500
Annual Fund Reminders (2 mailings only)	6 "	250
Vendor Solicitation	2 "	100
	119.5 days	$ 3,500

Activity: Meetings

All Development Committee Meetings (6 meetings)	25.5 days	
Alumni Board Meetings (10 meetings)	33 "	$ 500
Board Committee Meetings (10 meetings)	10 "	
	68.5 days	$ 500

General Administrative Support

Office supplies, equipment maintenance, miscellaneous alumni and development expenses.	0	$14,500

Summary:
Total Dollars: $57,975 programming
                                                        8,000 Archives

                                                  _____
                                                        $65,975

Total Work Days: 950 + 20% interruption
                                   time = 1138 days

Alumni Work Days: 343
Development
(alumni):   283.5
Development
(parent):   242.5 (including parent events)
Institution Activities: 80

Finally, staff places each program on a calendar that could be met with the staff available.

Activity Communications	1987												1988												1989	
	J	F	M	A	M	J	J	A	S	O	N	D	J	F	M	A	M	J	J	A	S	O	N	D	J	F
Alumni Quarterly	X			X			X			X			X		X		X		X		X		X			X
Annual Report								X												X						
Class Agent solicitation letters (excluding those who gave this year)								X												X						
Parent Newsletter	X				X				X				X				X				X					
Leadership Newsletter								X												X						
T.L.C. letter		X			X		X		X			X		X		X			X		X		X			
Planned giving general mailing												X	X	X												
Board Development Committee Meeting (including special gifts and planned giving)	X			X			X			X			X		X		X		X						X	
National Advisory Council meetings							X			X								X		X						
National Leadership Workshop							X											X								
REGIONAL ALUMNI ACTIVITY CYCLE																										
Regional Coordinator mailing to regional alumni including issue of Leadership Newsletter									X													X				

Activity Regional Alumni Activity Cycle (cont.)	1987 J	F	M	A	M	J	J	A	S	O	N	D	1988 J	F	M	A	M	J	J	A	S	O	N	D	1989 J	F
Announce activity calendar in Quarterly											X												X			
Regional Coordinator January letter of activity (3 days each region)	X												X												X	
Invitation mailings (2 days each region)		X												X												X
Conduct regional activities			|												|											
Post-activity mailings to no-shows (2 days each region)					X												X									
Post-competitive mailing to regionals (3 days each region)							X												X							
CLASS SECRETARY PROGRAM																										
Recruit National Class Secretary Chair	X																									
Recruit decade chair (3-year appointment)			|																							
Host decade chair workshop				X										X												
Recruit class secretary (2-year appointment)				|																						
Class secretary reports due (keyed to work calendar of the Quarterly)																		X								

Activity Class Secretary Program (cont.)	1987												1988												1989	
	J	F	M	A	M	J	J	A	S	O	N	D	J	F	M	A	M	J	J	A	S	O	N	D	J	F
Class secretary attends leadership workshop					X													X								
6-9 MONTHS **ALUMNI DIRECTORY** **(Published every 3 years)**																										
4-6 months Update bio information in alumni file																										
2-3 months Update present parent bio information						X																				
Announce program and timeline in spring Quarterly								X																		
Send letter to alum with bio info we have asking to update							X																			
Second request for update								X																		
Call those not responding									X																	
Update computer										X																
Computer generate list for typeset												X														
Publish directory as issue of the Quarterly													X													
18-MONTH **REUNION CLASS ACTIVITIES CALENDAR**																										
Class secretary conducts update of 5-year reunion classes	'86 Reunion Classes												'87 Reunion Classes													

Activity Reunion Class (cont.)	1987												1988												1989	
	J	F	M	A	M	J	J	A	S	O	N	D	J	F	M	A	M	J	J	A	S	O	N	D	J	F
Recruit reunion class chair			X												X											
Recruit reunion class activities committee				▮											X											
Recruit reunion class giving chair			X												X											
Recruit reunion class gift committee				▮											X											
Reunion class leadership attend leadership workshop							X											X								
Letter to class re: activities and giving goal								X												X						
Kickoff of reunion activities and solicitation (Homecoming)											X												X			
Solicitation of lead gifts									▮														▮			
Conduct reunion class phonathons											▮												▮			
Celebrate reunion and present class gift																		X								

Activity Annual Fund	1987												1988												1989	
	J	F	M	A	M	J	J	A	S	O	N	D	J	F	M	A	M	J	J	A	S	O	N	D	J	F
GENERAL CALENDAR																										
Enlist general chair (Honorary)			X												X											
Enlist lead gift leadership: Local alumni, parents, regional alumni, past parents, business and senior gift				|											X											
Enlist phonathon chairs: Alumni, parents, friends and senior gift				X												X										
Leadership attend leadership workshop Review and rate prospects Identify worker prospects						X												X								
Enlist lead gift workers							|													|						
Conduct lead gift worker update									X												X					
Mail first class agent letter									X												X					
Mail lead gift letter										X												X				
Solicit lead gift prospects												|												|		
Mail phonathon worker enlistment letter										X													X			
Conduct worker enlistment phonathon										X													X			
Conduct phonathons											|													|		

Activity General Calendar (cont.)	1987 J	F	M	A	M	J	J	A	S	O	N	D	1988 J	F	M	A	M	J	J	A	S	O	N	D	1989 J	F
Mail second class agent letter													X												X	
Mail third class agent letter														X												
Conduct mini-phonathons														X												X
Conduct final reminder phonathon															X											
CLASS AGENT ALUMNI PROGRAM																										
Enlist national class agent chair	X																									
Enlist decade chair (3-year term)				│																						
Enlist class agents (2-year term)			│ │																							
Class agents attend leadership workshop Review class for leadership Prepare letters for coming campaign							X																			
Mail first class agent letter									X																	
Mail second class agent letter													X												X	
Mail third class agent letter															X											
Class agents receive regular updates for preparation of thank you letter									▮	▮	▮	▮	▮	▮	▮	▮										

Activity Parents Annual Fund	1987												1988												1989	
	J	F	M	A	M	J	J	A	S	O	N	D	J	F	M	A	M	J	J	A	S	O	N	D	J	F
PARENT ORIENTATION EVENTS																										
4-LS, MS, US & senior gift co-sponsors with Headmaster, parents, Development Committee		│	│	│									│	│	│										
Enlist leadership—2 couples per class			│	│																						
Enlist parent phonathon chairs (one per school)			X													X										
Enlist senior gift chair	X													X												
Enlist senior gift committee			│											│	│	│										
Participation in leadership workshop Review prospects Identify worker prospects Set senior gift goal and project						X											X									
Lead gift workers participate in lead gift orientation and get prospect cards									X											X						
Mail first class agent letter								X												X						
Mail second class agent letter													X													X

Activity Parents Annual Fund (cont.)	1987												1988												1989	
	J	F	M	A	M	J	J	A	S	O	N	D	J	F	M	A	M	J	J	A	S	O	N	D	J	F
Mail third class agent letter															X											
Class agents receive regular updates to prepare thank you letters									■						■											

Activity Solict Major Donors	1987												1988												1989	
	J	F	M	A	M	J	J	A	S	O	N	D	J	F	M	A	M	J	J	A	S	O	N	D	J	F
Current CC Committee meetings to:	X	X	X	X	X	X	X	X																		
Conclude current $3M campaign																										
Enlist ongoing special gift committee		▮	▮	▮																						
Host first special gift committee leadership workshop						X											X									
Meet with 25- and 50-year reunion class leadership to rate prospects and set class gift goal and gift																										
Receive from Board special gift opportunities for coming year																										
Rate non-reunioning prospects																										
Take assignments																										
Participate with reunioning class leadership to solicit prospects									▮	▮	▮										▮	▮	▮			
Special Gift Committee #2									X														X			
Special Gift Committee #3													X											X		
Special Gift Committee #4																X										

PLANNED GIVING

Mailings are included on page one of the calendar. Other work will be responsive to solicitation centers such as special gifts, reunion class, and those who respond to the general or specific mailings assoc-iated with reunions. This program will be further developed when other components are affirmed.

10 Staff, equipment, space and budget

Staff

The development staff has a relationship with the governing board unlike any other staff. Their unique role in fulfilling institutional goals is to service the needs of the volunteer rather than the "client."

In most situations a board or other volunteer governing body sets a policy (e.g. to meet the special needs of working parents). That policy then carries with it a set of operational objectives (to offer an extended day care program). Staff is then hired to implement those objectives. In most situations, once policy is determined and the staff is hired, policy makers have little direct contact with staff, unless there are problems, until evaluation time.

The development professional should have a different relationship with policy makers and other volunteers, for not only does the volunteer set policy for the development office, but that same volunteer is responsible for implementation. The answer to the question, "Who is on first—staff or volunteer?" varies according to the stage of implementation. A simple statement of that shifting responsibility might be summed up as follows:

1. *Goal setting*—volunteers set goals based upon data provided by staff.

2. *Program design*—volunteers and staff work together to establish objectives.

3. *Program implementation*—staff directs and coordinates the work of key volunteers, who supervise the work of other volunteers in the identification, cultivation, and solicitation of prospective donors.

4. *Evaluation*—volunteers evaluate themselves and staff through analysis of data provided by staff.

Because of the shifting pattern of responsibility, the abilities of the advancement staff must go beyond command of basic skills and knowledge in a program area. The staff must possess an above average competence in people skills. Staff must intuitively know, for example, when to be assertive with program possibilities and when to let the volunteers struggle with the issues. Either alternative is chosen to promote volunteer ownership ahead of temporary program gains that might be available if the staff carried out programs instead of volunteers.

The advancement professional must be able to lead from the back of the room. To assume an inappropriate level of visibility is to assume responsibility for success while being dependent upon the volunteer's work to accomplish that success. The volunteers must always retain ultimate responsibility for the program. The staff supports and facilitates the volunteer's success. The advancement professional must have the knowledge to offer programs that will work and the interpersonal skills to enable the volunteer to master the program.

The development staff must avoid flaws in the information provided to the volunteer. Errors could be embarrassing to the worker and the prospect and could weaken the position of the foundation. Volunteers are volunteers, and should not be expected to remember detail. Rather they should be given the necessary information to accomplish their tasks.

That orientation to detail must also extend to maintenance of a work calendar. Often staff is the only one to fully understand the interdependence of one program upon another. Staff should sensitively communicate how one person's work enables another's to begin.

Two levels of staff are required within an advancement office—executive and support staff. Executive staff is composed of individuals with development experience and a clearly demonstrated record of accomplishments. In private secondary schools and smaller non-profit organizations such individuals generally carry the title director; in colleges and universities and larger non-profit institutions the title vice-president is normal.

The role of executive staff is to:

1. Serve as secretary and resource to the planning and goal setting process of the volunteer leadership.

2. Monitor the implementation of the program; identify problem areas and develop alternative strategies to compensate for emerging weaknesses.

3. Develop, with volunteers and support staff, strategies for implementing objectives identified by the volunteer leadership.

4. Provide essential training to volunteers to ensure the effectiveness of their work.

5. Support volunteer enlistment and solicitation calls.

6. Coordinate the work of support staff.

7. Ensure the effective maintenance of appropriate work calendars.

In smaller organizations, support staff generally means the secretary. As programs expand, support staff also expands and often includes specialists, hired by the job, day, or hour to strengthen specific program areas, such as publications, data entry, writers, researchers, and events managers. The role of the support staff is to:

1. See to the development, retention, and availability of pertinent data.

2. Prepare information and materials to support the cultivation, enlistment, and solicitation activities of the volunteers.

3. Facilitate an accurate and timely flow of information: volunteer to institution, volunteer to volunteer, institution to volunteer, and institution to community.

4. Ensure effective management of all program events.

When hiring initial staff, beware of overhiring at the top and then not supporting the system adequately at its base. The foundation of the program will rest on its ability to handle detail, such as mailings, constituency research, publications, public relations, data management, and event management. These activities, each time consuming, will require the largest investment of staff time. The most successful start up programs often begin with the hiring of a strong, experienced self-starting secretary who can organize data, set up the basic systems of the office, and begin the first steps in constituency identification and research.

The first risk in overhiring is that the person hired will not be able to accomplish the necessary tasks. If the first person on the job cannot type, problems will follow. However, paying someone $30,000—$40,000 to do simple data entry, even if that person can type, is poor management. Too much staff at the top with too little support staff causes inefficiency resulting from misplaced responsibilities.

Many of the responsibilities assigned to executive leadership can be "purchased separately." Firms exist that specialize in providing support to the development of the systems necessary to manage a data base and a phonathon. Likewise, some consulting firms specialize in board development, strategic planning, volunteer training, virtually everything up to and including on site program management. These firms, however, will not raise money— that is the job of the volunteer.

The most cost efficient way to begin is to hire as little of the most expensive staff and as much of the least expensive staff as is necessary to get the job done.

Significant strength can be realized by appointing a beloved teacher to begin your office. First, such a move may bring intimate knowledge of a group of graduating classes and their parents that could be invaluable in prospect identification and rating. Second, the proper appointment can bring legitimacy by association to a new idea.

Assuming that the teacher or administrator is new to development, a cost effective arrangement might be made where the teacher is involved in the development program part time and maintains a role in the classroom or administration, thus sharing the salary with another program. Providing executive leadership through a faculty member, the faculty member could work half time, supported by counsel. He or she should be encouraged to attend one or two training seminars, for new development officers can accomplish many goals. Supporting executive and volunteer leadership with a full time executive secretary and technicians, such as graphic designers hired by the hour, can provide a cost effective and well managed start-up staff.

Be cautious when hiring from within. The individual must stand up to the competition of an open search. Related experience in a position such as department head or director of special projects responsible for grants (public or private) will provide understanding of the district's programs and experience in management of personnel. However, some information concerning running a development program still must be learned or imported.

When to call and what to look for in a consultant

There are four basic stages in any venture: goal setting, design, implementation, and evaluation. Although the institution remains ultimately responsible for actions taken at every stage, outside consultants still can be of service.

Some moments to call on a consultant:

1. When an area of specialization is needed on a limited basis and it is not present in house.

2. When someone is needed to direct a short term program and the institution wishes to avoid the problems of training and dispersing staff at the conclusion of the program.

3. When all have reached an impasse and fresh ideas are needed.

4. When there is a perceived need for an evaluation by a disinterested party to identify potential program flaws before they become malignant.

The consultant, properly used during goal setting, design, and evaluation, can help ensure a cost effective program. Evaluate using consultants in light of their cost effectiveness.

Perhaps the greatest potential for the use of a consultant is during evaluation. Effectively designed and sensitively executed regular and summary evaluations can be instrumental in increasing efficiency and effectiveness.

Attention to process is vital—each step of any program must provide for proper "constituency buying in." To ensure success constantly monitor that "buying in" process. A consultant, not immersed in the minutiae of operations, can be effective in that monitoring process and provide significant input toward ensuring that mid-course corrections are identified and executed at the proper time in the life of the program.

What should a foundation look for in a consultant? First,

most foundations look to a consultant for knowledge on a given subject. It is appropriate to expect a high degree of sophistication in the particular area.

The most meaningful consultant to an organization will possess more than objective knowledge. Even the best consultant will not likely possess more objective data than the institution. Equally unlikely is that the consultant will be able to accomplish anything that personnel living in the community could not master given the proper ambience.

For others, the ultimate consultant is one who can reach beyond everyday knowledge by drawing on previous experience to arrive at a solution. It is true that through experience one masters the practical realities of a discipline. There is a direct relationship between the experience of a designer and the strength of the design.

However, today's problems cannot always be solved with yesterday's solutions.

As important as knowledge and previous experience are, two other attributes are essential. First, the consultant must have the ability to intentionally, kindly, and thoroughly "upset the apple cart." Then, through creatively reassembling the data, the consultant must be a catalytic agent in the design and implementation of appropriate solutions. The consultant's outsider quality provides an objective evaluation that facilitates the development of effective solutions.

Finally, the consultant must be able to interpret what is being said between the lines. The consultant must unearth the real questions that should be asked. Only then can meaningful answers be found. The skilled consultant can hasten the search for those questions and ensure their thoroughness.

Equipment

The foundation must be well presented on paper, which requires an investment in good typing and reproduction equipment. Recognizing the cyclical, repetitive, and data centered nature of many of the functions of a development office, seriously consider an up front investment in a data/ word processing system that will likely pay for itself in the first year.

As a volunteer centered organization, there will be temptations to seek contributions to furnish and equip the office. Hand-me-downs are fine provided they fit. To avoid embarrassing a donor/volunteer, and to avoid collecting a room full of useless equipment be specific about needs. Determine through thorough and responsible planning what the needs of the foundation are and will be, and then make that plan and its specific needs known to your constituents as part of the solicitation process.

Space

Location of the foundation office makes a statement about the foundation's intended role in the community. Proximity to the school board and superintendent's offices will indicate a mutually supportive relationship and will facilitate communication and in-kind district support.

In most situations, however, some separation should be maintained so the foundation may grow into a strength of its own. The foundation must be an independent agency responsible to the community through its own volunteer board and governance.

In appointment, the foundation should compare favorably with the offices of the superintendent. The leadership of the community must pass through this space. It should not be ostentatious, but it should be comfortable and tasteful.

The ideal initial space would have two offices with one large enough to serve as a small meeting room accommodating eight to ten people. The setting would be informal, with sufficient space for a table, the director's desk and work space.

Increasingly, space is defined by the way one enters it electronically. The foundation should have its own phone line for clarity in accounting and image.

Budget

The development of initial budgets is as difficult as it is crucial. It is difficult because there is no history to build upon. It is crucial because budgets create their own force and in part direct the future development of the foundation and its programs. In addition, prospects want to see trial budgets to determine whether the project is feasible before making an investment.

Budgets must come directly out of the mission statement. What are the goals of the foundation? What will they cost to fulfill? How much must be invested to reach these goals? Who would not invest $30,000—$50,000 if that investment would in five years open a valve to a new pipeline of support that would generate over $100,000 each year? It will take dollars to begin.

Three subjective factors determine the shape of initial budgets:

1. Where does the foundation want to be in five years in terms of:
   a. Spendable program dollars.
   b. Percent of total income invested in operations?

2. How much is the leadership, enlisted at the time of the development of the initial budgets, willing to invest to get things going?

3. What is the appropriate cost of opening the doors?

Some basic management concepts and realities have to be accommodated.

1. Management should be in the office eight hours a day. Less time will create difficult situations. New volunteers

who lack the knowledge to answer prospect's questions must have someone to consult. Often a new volunteer is asked to participate before that individual has any understanding of the mission of the foundation.

2. Although volunteers will make the foundation successful, staff must play a number of critical roles. A sacrifice on staff wages will jeopardize the development of the foundation. Able people managers with a track record of accomplishment in the support of volunteers are not inexpensive. Yet, to have anyone with less than strong organizational and people skills is to begin the race with one broken leg. Volunteers can be counted on for many tasks, but maintaining the kind of records the foundation will need to grow is best accomplished by staff, who can be held accountable in ways volunteers cannot.

Operations vs. program

Prospects generally ask solicitors, "How much of my dollar goes to the cause?" There is the general perception that people are unwilling to give to fund raising costs. Although this is often true, it is also true that prospects will give if the program is successful in meeting an important need.

One way to handle what may seem to be inordinately high initial costs is to package initial start up costs as an investment in meeting the problem. Identify a "start up fund" to which people might make a gift, and then invite a few key donor prospects to invest in the future by ensuring the quality of the beginning. This fund should provide a base of support from a few as the foundation develops its broad base of donors. Draw a five year plan reflecting the development and transition to the point where all operations can be absorbed within the annual income.

Start up funding and operating funds distribution chart

Year	Start up fund	Annual gifts to operations	Annual gifts to program
year #1	100%	—0—	—0—
year #2	66%	16%	16%
year #3	33%	33%	33%
year #4	—0—	30%	70%
year #5	—0—	20%	80%

Assuming that first year operating costs are $30,000, and that these costs remain constant throughout the five year period by refocusing spending, the expenditures in programs in year five could be $80,000 or more.

In year 2 the projected annual fund income would be $20,000, year 3—$40,000, year 4—$60,000 and year 5—$100,000. More ambitious goals would mean a lower percentage going to administration and fund raising.

Defining administrative vs. program costs

It is not true in development that ". . .a rose by any other name will smell as sweet." Be certain when developing initial budgets that the chart of accounts reflects the accurate balance between administration and program. Administrative costs cannot be assigned to any particular program such as the annual audit, basic phone, support for the board of trustees. Program costs are dollars invested in the pursuit of accomplishing goals. A list of the foundation's programs could include:

1. *Communications and public information.* Programs run in the areas of public relations, alumni/parent publications, general image development.

2. *Constituency involvement.* Programs that strengthen the district through direct involvement of parents, alumni, and friends of the district.

3. *Special program grants.* Grants given to individuals and institutions that strengthen the educational programs of the district.

4. *Recognition of excellence.* Events and activities sponsored or managed by the foundation that recognize exceptional achievement in support of the programs of the district.

Fund raising costs include expenditures made while supporting solicitation, gift recording, and gift acknowledgement.

A similar kind of specificity would assist in the solicitation of start up funds. Do not ask for $60,000 over three years to start the foundation. Ask individuals to give dollars to cover the cost of filing charters, 501C3 applications, developing a data base, tracking alumni, supporting initial reunion activities, running a series of community leaders orientation sessions, developing a more readable parents newsletter, and developing a volunteer corps to serve the special needs of the district.

General rules of thumb

The National Association of Independent Schools each year publishes development related statistics. In 1984 it found that fund raising costs, including salary and program expenses for development, alumni and parent relations, and publications and public relations averaged 23.3 percent of giving income.

In addition, salaries generally represent 50 to 75 percent of the cost of the development program.

11 Installing and maintaining an appropriate data base

The first rule for effective solicitation: know and be a part of the cause. The second rule: know the prospect. What an individual donor has given in the past is certainly basic information to have available, but it is only the beginning. It may not reflect the donor's true potential.

When assessing potential it may be important to know that five years ago the prospect wrote an editorial in the local paper praising the work being done with learning disabled children. Two years ago that same person corresponded with the superintendent asking if more could be done in that area. This information could form the basis for a specific appeal to purchase needed equipment for which there are no budgeted funds. Knowing who to call with special needs is the first step in meeting these needs.

Defining a data base

When establishing any data base there are three issues to address. (1) What kind of data is important to keep? (2) How does one keep that information? (3) Where does one find current information?

A development program has four specific tasks that must

be supported by accurate information—communication, volunteer enlistment, solicitation, and program evaluation.

The first area of information to be retained supports the first stage of cultivation. Obviously, any program of information dissemination must maintain accurate formal names, addresses, and phone numbers.

The goal will be always to communicate in a personal way. Therefore, maintain additional listings that identify how the individual wishes to be addressed in more personal situations. It will be impossible to convince a prospect that they have a unique role and responsibility within the district if their name is continually mishandled. A prospect is not likely to seriously read or listen to information if it does not include the prospect's correct name.

It is often important to retain a number of addresses and phone numbers: home, mailing, summer/winter, and office.

If the data management system employed can accommodate the information, maintaining a record of recent communications or a contact chronicle can be valuable in analyzing the effectiveness of specific programs. It would be particularly important to chronicle any mail solicitation. Cross referencing such information with giving records will clearly identify the most effective type and time of solicitation for each prospect.

Much of the foundation work will have to be accomplished by volunteers. Remember, strong giving follows involvement. To facilitate effective volunteer involvement, it is necessary to know several kinds of information about potential workers. First, what have they done for the district or foundation in the past? Although this may be obvious information to retain, most program managers never adequately plan for their departure by keeping accurate and sufficient records of current activities.

The second type of information to be retained is, what does the individual do for other organizations? Few people invest all their volunteer activity in one place. Knowing what a volunteer does for another institution may give a clue to what they might be asked to do next for the foundation/district.

Family situation can often provide clues to a nominating committee. Young children in the home bring special concerns. Teenagers at home make some activities easier and others impossible. Family members with special needs also create special parent concerns and willingness to become involved. Vocational and educational activities and changes may signal a potential involvement opportunity or restriction that must be observed.

Solicitation calls for a comprehensive understanding of the prospect. The reason is not so the solicitor can better manipulate the prospect, but so that the needs and concerns of the donor might be met. "What might the donor hope to accomplish through this foundation?" is the root question. All of the above information can and will give clues to the answer.

The following is a representative list of information to consider retaining on each prospect:

1. Name

2. Addresses

3. Phone numbers

4. Classification—alumnus, parent, student, etc.

5. Family information

6. Employment information

7. Other community activities

8. Educational background

9. District/foundation volunteer activities

10. Giving record including:
    a. Total lifetime giving to date
    b. Number of gifts, years of support

    c. Largest gift to date

    d. Date of largest gift

    e. Designation of largest gift

    f. Last six gifts including date, designation, amount, type of solicitation

    g. Pledge, date made, and designation

11. Copies of all personal correspondence with the foundation

12. Clippings of media recognition

13. Programs/accounts of any programs recognizing support

14. Call report forms of other volunteer/staff contact.

Program evaluation is often overlooked. When an attempt is made it is generally undertaken with little or no data upon which to make judgments and usually focuses only on the "bottom line." The assumption is, "We met our goal so the program must be all right." Such an evaluation rarely considers the potential of individual programs, nor does it encourage innovation, and it can in fact limit growth.

To assemble sufficient data, keep careful records on each program as to: 1) How many individuals were prospects? 2) How many participated? 3) What was the level of participation? 4) What were the problems or supports that influenced the outcome? 5) How did this year's performance compare with previous years?

Managing a data base

The greatest deterrent to keeping good records is the lack of proper mechanisms to maintain the appropriate files. Two types of files are necessary: computerized records and paper files.

First, if the district cannot make available on line data processing, consider purchasing a stand alone system.

This may seem to be an exorbitant initial expense; however, since such a system will no doubt have word processing capability for little or no additional cost, the potential labor savings could pay for the system. More important, in the early months and years tremendous amounts of data will be stored.

Begin with proper equipment and software to avoid spending excessive time and dollars later entering all the data. Initial data entry will be accomplished as you proceed. In addition, you will have the benefits of automated data management from the beginning.

Data kept best on a computer is information that facilitates broad base communication, giving information, family information that seldom changes, such as children, education and vocational information, and coded information of volunteer activities within the district or foundation.

Exercise caution when considering setting up automated data management systems. A common error is trying to develop an automated system that keeps all the important information when tracking the giving and activities of the largest prospect in the file. This simply is not possible. Unless the constituency is large and active the kind of detail that must be maintained on major prospects can not efficiently be done on computer.

Therefore, in addition to an automated data base for the management of the bulk of the donors and other constituents, anticipate maintaining paper files on 20 to 50 percent of your people. In these files can be stored correspondence, newspaper clips, call report forms, and memos from staff concerning activities.

Finding the data

Data gathering is the essential first step to success. Initial leadership will determine the success of the first ten years. It is imperative that enlistments and prospect lists are based on the broadest and most accurate data culled from the broadest prospect pool possible. One must know who the best prospects are before enlistment begins.

The questions that bother most are where to find such information and how to begin its collection? There are services that one can use to locate missing alumni. The better ones tend to be expensive.

Begin the research by seeking the help and involvement of volunteers. Contact local associations of archivists, genealogists, newspaper research offices, and ask that they identify available resources to facilitate the development of verified addresses, etc. One approach followed by some private schools includes class projects requiring students to interview older alumni, who were identified through old yearbooks.

Plenty of information is actually available. The apparent dearth of information is generally due to a lack of efficient collection. Stress to your volunteers and staff the importance of promptly filling out "call report forms" on every contact made. Hire a good self-starting secretary with strong organizational skills. Provide a two day training seminar including trips to several private schools or college development offices. These steps will create an effective office of constituency research serving both volunteer recruitment and eventually the solicitation and evaluation needs of the foundation and the district.

What can a computer do within a development office?

Most of the functions of a development office require the thorough completion of standardized procedures involving the management of data relevant to the solicitation, receipt, and acknowledgement of gifts. Most standardized procedures can be done more efficiently and accurately on a computer than by hand.

The management of data within a development program is relatively simple. However, those simple tasks often require time consuming reformatting of basic information that the institution already has but in a different form. Such a situation is ideal for automation.

What can automated data management mean?

It can mean improved efficiency and greater accuracy of accounting functions. Its greatest contribution to accuracy lies in the fact that instead of having to enter the same information in several places to accommodate the multiple accounting and reporting functions, one entry will simultaneously perform multiple informational, recording, and procedural functions.

Without automation, the relatively simple process of recording a gift generally requires the entry of each gift in five separate places, and the hand retyping of the donor's address twice. To use that information, one must use one or more of those files, handling each gift again to develop the summary or list required by the program. With automation one will enter the gift only once and all other manipulation of that information in the future will be accomplished electronically.

For example: Recording a gift will require entering, one time, the date (which may be automatically filled in with that work day's date), amount of gift, designation of gift, and solicitor or type of solicitation.

That one data entry will make possible:

1. Automatic crediting of each gift to a specific outstanding pledge and maintenance of individual donor history,

2. Automatic crediting of each gift to any designated fund within the foundation,

3. Automatic update and maintenance of the income history and donor participation within each fund,

4. Automatic update of solicitor's progress,

5. Automated receipt and acknowledgement process and materials preparation,

6. Automated "anniversary of the gift" renewal procedures and materials preparation,

7. Automated monthly updates on membership renewal progress and tracking of LYBUNTS, progress of special gift solicitation, and preparation of reminders for outstanding pledges,

8. Automated preparation of year end (or periodic) donor/membership lists to facilitate volunteer enlistment, program clean up, evaluation, and preparation of honor roll of supporters and friends,

9. Automated assistance in tracking and analysis of last year's volunteer worker effectiveness,

10. Automated assistance in preparing the coming campaign's enlistment materials,

11. Automated assistance in preparing coming campaign's prospect list,

12. Automated assistance in preparing individual solicitation materials for all members and prospects,

13. Automated assistance in preparing special or specific solicitations based upon the individual's personal involvement with the foundation,

14. Automated preparation of bank deposits, daily transmittal logs, and hard copy files where desirable.

In one form or another anticipate doing all the above tasks and functions at the beginning. Most of the tasks and reports listed require preparation time that without auto-mation will take hours or days.

Without automation, each of the above functions and re-ports require:

1. Hand sorting individual giving history cards,
2. Hand reformatting data,
3. Hand collation of that information with compar-ative or supplemental data drawn from other sources, such as last year's campaign work sheets, accounts, ledgers, or biographical infor-mation files,
4. Hand preparation of reports and generally repet-itive materials.

Without automation much of the development office's time is spent not in collecting new information or in running programs, but in reformatting information already ob-tained and in executing mundane and repetitive tasks. It is not uncommon for institutions to take days and weeks in the preparation of year end donor lists to ensure their accu-racy. Other reports, such as worker progress reports, monthly updates on progress or problems, never get pro-duced on time.

With automation, *all* of the above functions and reports would take minutes or at the most hours from conception to printed report, and all reports would be based on up-to-the-minute information.

How much will all this cost?

Most software that is being developed will run on an IBM PC with hard disk or its equivalent. The *New York Times* listed such equipment around $3,000. A letter quality printer will also need to be purchased, costing approximately $2,000. Depending on other peripherals purchased, such as addi-tional work stations, the total cost could run as high as

$6,500–$7,500. Software costs could be as low as $1,000 or run as high as $10,000 for a development package.

As there is always a potential to over spend, there is also a danger in underinvesting. In such an instance, an investment could fall short of meeting the needs of the foundation. Also, a less expensive installation is generally more difficult to work with and has fewer compatible software.

What, besides supporting development, will this program do?

In addition to serving the needs of the development office, a good development program tracks volunteer activity, and the special interests of each constituent. Likewise, it retains related information, such as an individual's involvement in other related institutions, when gathering the data.

Such data supports the foundation's advocacy and information/educational programs by facilitating the preparation of special interest mailings through automated label preparation, and the maintenance of a chronicle of contact with each constituent. By retaining the capability to add categories of information, this program also can expand to meet the future needs of the foundation.

With the purchase of additional software, the foundation will be able to automate the accounting functions of the foundation and provide word processing capability that can be operated separate from, or integrated with, any of the foundation's operational or personnel data bases.

12 A case study—
The Albany Academy

I am using a private institution for this case study for two reasons. First, few public schools have a proven track record in the broad base program one expects to see in the private sector. School districts and communities initiating development programming generally concentrate on corporate and foundation solicitation rather than individual solicitation. Those that do focus on individuals have too little history to build on.

Second, I use this particular school because the nature of the problems within The Albany Academy correspond to the major benefits the public schools can expect from establishing a foundation or internal development office.

1. A more aware and happier constituency.
2. Greater volunteer participation and pride.
3. More money for program.
4. A clearly identified, growing and committed support base.

The Albany Academy is a celebrated institution that will in 1988 observe its 175th birthday. It has experienced periods of great strength and times of special challenge. As with most institutions, the 1960s and '70s provided one of those times of trial. During those years giving and enrollment declined, bringing stress to the administration and board.

From 1979 to 1985, however, its enrollment increased from 419 to 505 on the way to a planned 550 by 1989. Giving also rose from $45,000 to over $800,000 in 1984-85, excluding bequests. Including bequests the 1985-86 total exceeded $1,000,000. In the next three to five years annual gift income goals will be maintained at a steady $750,000 or more.

There is really very little difference in solving the development problems for any institution that has been instrumental in the lives of its constituency. Alumni, parents, and community members are such constituencies. In public or private schools, the same loyalties can be kindled and the appeal for support can be as compelling.

The following charts show the development of this program in measurable statistics. (See next page.)

Building upon the Albany Academy program goals as a model, I will attempt to indicate how the same goals might be approached in the public school sector.

Defining and redefining who we are: Year 1/1979–80

Albany Academy development, like many of the Albany Academy's systems, was underproducing in relation to the dollars being invested. A series of unbalanced budgets left little money to spend on programs as nonacademic as alumni relations and development. The lack of direction of the institution was displayed in the development program through an ongoing feud between the development office and the office of the Alumni Secretary.

Many attitudes had to be changed and patterns of support redeveloped before significant gift income could be expected.

Because of the lack of cooperation between offices and because of a lack of continuity in the leadership of the devel-

Albany Academy seven year development statistics

Year	79-80	80-81	81-82	82-83	83-84	84-85	Projected 85-86	Alb Acad Totals	National Statistics
# Staff	1½	3	3	3½	4¼	4	4½		
$ Staff	22,000	30,000	33,000	37,000	40,000	50,000	90,000	$ 302,000	
$ Program	18,000	19,000	20,000	26,000	20,000	23,000	56,000	$ 182,000	
Capital	-0-	3,000	15,000	80,000	95,000	25,000	-0-	$ 218,000	
Total Cost	$ 40,000	$ 52,000	$ 68,000	$143.00	$ 155,000	$ 98,000	$ 146,000	$ 702,000	
Gift $ AG	102,000	122,000	147,000	130,000	127,000	147,000	175,000	$ 950,000	
Gift $ CC	-0-	-0-	-0-	117,000	443,000	675,000	475,000	$1,710,000	
Estate Gift	-0-	1,200,000	-0-	-0-	-0-	-0-	350,000	$1,550,000	
Total Gift	$102,000	$1,322,000	$147,000	$247,000	$ 570,000	$ 822,000	$1,000,000	$4,210,000	
Cost as % of Gift	39%	4%	46%	57%	27%	12%	16%	16.7%	15%-21%
# Gift AF									
Alumni	507	654	808	745	705	839			
Parents	96	158	154	191	159	228			
Avg Gift AF									
Alumni	$150.00**	$ 83.00	$ 68.00	$ 78.00	$80.00	$81.00			$103
Parent	$ 87.00	$ 61.00	$ 69.00	$ 70.00	$67.00	$82.00			$320
% Participation AF									
Alumni	23%	32%	38%	33%	30%	36%			42%
Parent	28%	39%	36%	45%	35%	51%			67%

AG = All restricted and unrestricted gifts given with the intent the gift would be spent in the year of the donation.
AF = All unrestricted gifts given in support of the operating budget for that year.
CC = gifts given to support a specific capital fund appeal.
** = average gift high due to $30,000 challenge gift.

opment office, data and records had been sloppily maintained.

Public School. Raising gift income from the private sector for a public school will take making friends, changing minds, and raising consciousness among each potential support group. This requires communicating with friends and then involving them in building a stronger school district. A great deal of the first year will be spent in preparation (filing of state charters and applying for tax exempt status.)

Year 1/1979–80

Albany Academy Program	Public School Program
Read the existing files and reformatted data into standard development format.	Begin gathering lists of alumni, key parents, and potential friends.
Maintained alumni publication and events schedule.	Begin publication program highlighting district success and volunteer activities.
Converted data base to computer.	Begin the development of a data base.
Secured challenge gift to stimulate giving.	Enlist permanent board of trustees.
Ran mail Annual Fund solicitation.	Solicit trustees and 25–50 key prospects for start up funds.
Headmaster ran parent class parties.	Conduct community information sessions through PTO and back-to-school nights.
Reestablished donor recognition dinner.	Conduct first annual fund solicitation via mail among 500–1,000 prospects identified through initial research.

Developing and improving constituency relations: Year 2/1980–81

Albany Academy. Times of stress can leave a trail of mistrust. The institution should build the confidence of its constituents (alumni, parents, and friends), not only of its users (students). Already in place within the Academy was a tradition of loyalty. The Academy had nurtured this through the years by providing its constituencies with information and opportunities for involvement.

A new attitude about volunteering in the school setting had to be developed. More openness in management and a new placement of volunteer energy into appropriate activities were needed.

Public School. A lively discussion could ensue from the question, "Which is more difficult to overcome, inertia or ill will?" What ill will the Academy may have generated through self- and public-image confusion, a public school foundation can match in inertia because of no image at all.

Much of year two will be spent answering the basic question, "Who are you?"

Year 2/1980–81

Albany Academy Program	Public School Program
Headmaster hosted parent meetings with each class.	School and foundation co-sponsor expanded community information sessions with key community leadership.
Stronger emphasis on parent open house type functions.	Make grants out of income from initial year annual fund appeal.
Conducted the following alumni activities: Homecoming reception Alumni mid-winter dinner Spring Alumni Day Began alumni regional meetings Hosted alumni-faculty party.	Publish formal "case for support."
Established office of public relations—1/2 time.	Secure challenge gift to inspire giving and expand base of support.
Published three issues of alumni magazine and one honor role of donors and annual appeal.	Conduct second annual fund appeal via mail.
Initiated annual fund phonathons.	Initiate phonathons as means to expand donor base.
Conducted feasibility study testing readiness for a capital campaign.	Initiate alumni program with fall 'young alumni sports day' at Thanksgiving time and all alumni reunion featuring five year reunion classes in spring.
Board of Trustees established all constituency long range planning committees.	Conduct community-wide feasibility study to gather information to assist the foundation's long range planning process.

Strengthening/initiating fund raising through effective rating: Year 3/1981–82

Albany Academy. The Academy was recognizing the need for an infusion of new capital to accomplish its mission. The Long Range Planning Committee was identifying both programs and facilities that needed attention. However, the feasibility study indicated that the prospects were not ready to provide new capital in the amounts needed.

The quality of the Academy's programs was still of concern among alumni and parents. They questioned whether the problems of the past had been overcome. Despite attempts to open the information gates, the average prospect still felt excluded from the decision making process.

Although individuals were willing to give, their contributions had to increase to meet the school's gift income needs. Those who were giving $100 had to think in terms of $250 for the Annual Fund and $5,000 for capital purposes. Those giving $2,500 each year would have to think of $250,000 for the capital campaign. The giving potential was within the institution, but a great deal had to be done before those who could provide leadership in giving would be ready.

Public School. By year three, schools that have done their work well will have developed a base of support. It will also be likely that a first success will have whetted the appetite of those involved. "If we can do this much with what we have, think what we could do if only we could . . . ." When that sentiment is heard, it means the base exists to begin considering a different level of cultivation and expectations.

Year 3/1981–82

Albany Academy Program
Initiated individual solicitation Lead Gift Program within the Annual Fund.

Public School Program
Initiate lead gift program to support annual fund.

Albany Academy Program	Public School Program
Initiated more extensive and formal Annual Report sent to the whole constituency.	Establish donor club program for annual fund.
Appointed Capital Campaign Steering Committee. Their charge was to develop a plan for a CC and enlist the key leadership.	Publish foundation annual report including honor role of donors.
Conducted an institution-wide talent search to help identify leadership prospects.	Initiate solicitation by employing volunteer leadership from each school building.
Conducted phonathons. Expanded number of nights of phoning.	Initiate special alumni involvement opportunities program.
Maintained traditional alumni programming.	Expand phonathons.
Maintained standard publications and public relations program.	Formalize classroom grants program.
	Provide coordination to district-wide volunteer program.

First major program expansion: Year 4/1982–83

Albany Academy. The Long Range Plan was now coming into focus. Needs were defined. Internally the institution had regained balance. Volunteers were coming forward and accepting new responsibilities with enthusiasm. Steps were taken to fully integrate the development and alumni offices. It was time to begin a major external relations offensive.

Early in the year the trustees affirmed that, rather than athletics, extra curricular activities, and other areas that also needed support, the capital campaign should focus on the academic program needs of the school. That decision provided focus and emphasis to the campaign.

Public School. In the ideal world, this would be the first year the foundation would exist without outside support in the form of start up funding. But, you are no longer the new kid on the block. A new era of legitimacy should be dawning. It is time to assume leadership.

Year 4/1982–83

Albany Academy Program	Public School Program
Maintained Annual Fund with greater emphasis on lead gift programs.	Maintain annual fund with more emphasis placed on lead gift program
Moved phonathons to a newly developed in house facility.	Expand phonathons.
Developed capital campaign plan.	Foundation board meet with school board and identify portions of district long range plan it will assume responsibility for.
Board approved Capital Campaign Case Statement.	Conduct full constituency rating.
Staff prepared 15 min. slide/audio presentation of needs.	Identify special gift, $5,000 and above prospect list.
Enlisted Capital Campaign Cabinet.	Enlist special gift committee.
Began solicitation of trustees and key campaign leadership.	Add foundation leadership newsletter to regular publications.
Set $3M goal after 18 trustees pledged over $750K. Began major gift solicitation with a working goal of 50% of goal by public kick off next fall.	Develop slide/audio show on foundation activities and goals.
Conducted full constituency rating. Moved data management in house.	Sponsor donor club banquet.
Maintained publication and public relations effort. Added a capital campaign newsletter to publications schedule.	
Established an Alumni National Advisory Board.	
Enhanced external relations through opening art gallery and expanded academic recognition program.	

A program comes of age:
Year 5/1983–84

Albany Academy. In many ways the past four years had been preparation for this year and the years to come. Sights had been elevated. Information had been distributed. Volunteer leadership had been enlisted. Giving leadership had been secured. All was ready for a major push. In addition to the Capital Campaign the Academy added one more major community relations activity.

Recognizing that the Capital Campaign would go on for some time and that there would be a need for so-called public moments to punctuate the solicitation period, the Academy decided to sponsor a five year series of events identified as "anniversary gifts." These gifts would be made to the community in recognition of the Academy's own 175th birthday to be celebrated at the end of the campaign.

The first gift would be given at the time of the campaign kick off. It would be the commissioning of a new symphony premiered by the Albany Symphony Orchestra. The inspiration for the symphony would be the works of Hermann Melville, an alumnus of the school.

SECTION THREE—

Specific program management support

13 Developing the case for support

Significant gift income is generated in response to a worthy cause. Indeed, without a cause there is no constituency or reason for anyone to give.

The case statement is the presentation of that cause in any form. It must encapsulate the mission, history, strengths, needs, potential, and vision of the district.

The process the foundation uses in developing the case for support will determine the value of the final product. The most beneficial product will be expressed as much in the positive attitudes and commitment of the volunteers as the professional appearance of the case on the printed page.

Writing the case statement is only part of a larger program of total institutional advancement. Not only must the final product express the advancement goals of the district's development program, it must present these goals in the context of a specific tradition and program, and articulate the vision of a specific group of volunteers and prospects.

Volunteer ownership must begin with the formulation of the plan (long range planning), proceed through defining specific goals for programs, administration, and financing, and not stop until implementation is completed. Therefore, volunteer participation and input will be vital to the development of the case. It must state goals and outline plans for the future. Only when volunteer ownership is clear in the minds of the solicitor and the prospect, will the donor be comfortable with the investment and satisfied with the outcome of the project.

When writing the case for support of a new cause, volunteer involvement becomes even more important. We have no precedent to rely on; no issues of the past from which to learn. To replace experience, use information on the prospect's attitudes gained from interviews with the prospect base.

Attitude Survey

What questions must be answered before prospects will consider contributing money to public education? Present that question to those capable of giving the gifts necessary to fill the top donor categories of the scale of gifts, chapter 3.

Gather that information through a contract with development counsel or through a survey conducted by volunteers. Or maybe consider requesting a local college or university that has a department of statistics, sociology, public administration, or marketing to consider such a study as a thesis project.

If volunteers or a university group are employed to conduct the survey, consider commissioning an independent evaluation of the questionnaire, and study procedures to be conducted by professional development counsel. Make available counseling to the volunteers or university throughout the project by providing information specific to the field of development and institutional advancement.

The following is a questionnaire that might be given to select prospects to measure their feelings after giving to the district. Individual questions would vary according to the constituency characteristics.

Use of such a questionnaire must be accompanied by a

brief (two page) summary of the case for support. If the interviews are conducted personally, the case should be sent with the letter that requests the interview. Otherwise it should be sent with the questionnaire.

Sample Attitude Survey Questionnaire

Classification of interviewee: Alumnus   Trustee   Administrator   Faculty

Have you ever asked for money on behalf of the school district?
        SOURCE: Individual   HOW MUCH: $_____
                Foundations $_____
                Corporation $_____

Have you given personally or in the name of your company or foundation to the school district or any other public supported institution? Y N
Have you ever been asked to? Y N

Would you be willing to tell me where the gift you gave fell in the overall pattern of your personal charities?
Near the top middle lower 1/3

What questions did you have to satisfy for your prospects and/or yourself prior to giving?_____
_____
_____

Had they been answered differently would the level of giving been different? How? ____
_____
_____

What is the key prospect question? _____
_____
_____

What is the district's strongest selling point? _____
_____
_____

What three to five adjectives would you project the average prospect would include in a description of the district? _____
_____
_____

How would your description vary from the norm and why? _____

_____

_____

How would you describe the relationship between the administration, including key deans, etc., and the volunteer leadership of:

Alumni _____

_____

Trustees _____

_____

Leadership of the region's charitable community _____

_____

If you could change one thing about district schools what would it be? _____

_____

If you were going to train someone to solicit for the district what would you want them to know before they set out? _____

_____

What two topics must be included in a case for support of the district? _____

_____

Please think of other charities that you support—what is the common denominator among them that inspires your support? _____

_____

What do you feel must be done to correct the image of the district schools? You are asked to answer this question assuming that money is not a consideration, you have a blank check, what would you do? _____

_____

Outline of the case statement

The components of the case statement are essentially the same as the components of a prospectus seeking to inform and interest potential investors in a commercial venture. This should reinforce the fact that a solicitation is really a business contact and should be initiated with the same dedication and forethought as any other important project. Each element of the case must be adequately developed to answer basic prospect questions.

The case statement must illustrate and develop proofs to

the two fundamental equations that are in the mind of every donor:

(Worthy cause) + (Meaningful tradition) + (Current strengths) = *vision of a stronger tomorrow*

(Realistic plan) + (Donor strength) + (Personal commitment) = *success*

(Worthy cause)

Include a mission statement that answers in five to ten brief sentences the question: "Why are you here?" It may be a rewording of the statement of purpose filed with the state at the time you received your charter or your tax exempt status from the Internal Revenue Service. Later, when developing funding for a specific large program or facility, the statement of mission may focus more on the project and less on the overall foundation goals.

> The XXX Foundation exists to provide the citizens of Zzz School District with a vehicle through which they might invest personal charitable dollars in the lives and maturation of the youth of Zzz.
>
> Building on the district's current strength, the foundation intends to provide a "Fund for Excellence" by making available to the district program, staff, and at times facilities that otherwise would not be available through public funds. It is intended that the dollars given through the XXX Foundation will augment, not replace, tax or other public support.
>
> The XXX Foundation is a tax exempt community based institution with a self-perpetuating board of directors.

+ *(Meaningful tradition)*

A history section must present in five to seven brief paragraphs what you have done. Resist the tendency to overwrite this section. It is not intended to provide the reader with the definitive history of the community's roots or serve as a forum for the writer to chronicle the accomplishments of a superintendent or anyone else. Write this section to provide a backdrop to a request for action. Thus, the history section must be a recap of the excellence of the past that provides a motivation for the future.

People stories rather than dates provide the most motivation for they illustrate not only where the institution has come from, but why it exists. Donors want to contribute to a winning situation. Tradition is an integral part of a winner, and it enables the bridging of periods of trial.

+ *(Current strengths)*

No matter how lofty the mission or noble the history it is the ability of the institution to wisely invest today that builds donor confidence. Descriptions of the programs can either establish the basis for investment in a strong tomorrow, or make a plea for a gift to help right a wrong. People invest in excellence and give token gifts to needs. Pride of success promotes a willingness to invest.

This section must establish the district as an institution worthy of investment by demonstrating effective use of the resources available.

= A vision of a stronger tomorrow

Any projected program or change can be presented as either today's need or tomorrow's excellence. The goal of the case statement is to illustrate how proposed changes will produce excellence. Do not tell people what they must repair but how they can support a stronger tomorrow.

This section must illustrate how this project fulfills the mission statement. It must be consistent with the traditions of the past. It must build upon and extend current strengths.

As with other sections of the case statement, avoid an extensive presentation. Leaving the prospect with questions often provides conversation for the solicitation call.

Ultimately two versions of this will be needed. The prospects will need a brief version to attract attention and provide a summary of the vision behind the appeal. A second, longer version, will provide the solicitor with the data necessary to answer the prospect's questions.

Above all others, this section must have the approval and ownership of the foundation trustees, campaign committee, and the school board. Involving them in its development, as discussed earlier, will go a long way toward building that ownership.

(Realistic plan)

How excellence will be achieved must be explained to any serious prospect. Good ideas are only that until a plan of implementation is in place. Where will the money come from? How will be it be solicited? How will it be distributed? How will the programs funded be evaluated? The plan must be understood and believed by the prospects if they are to give.

+ *(Donor strength)*

Before presenting the prospect with a request for a specific commitment, illustrate the success achieved to date. It is easier to persuade people to join a winning team than to persuade them to start one. Success in enlisting volunteers to work, and early success in solicitation, provides the best reason to believe that goals can be achieved.

+ *(Personal commitment)*

To "close the sale" the case and the solicitor must answer the prospect's question, "What must I do for us to achieve success?"
= **SUCCESS**

Writing the case for support

Voice

The case for support is written from the platform of the trustees—the ones who spend the money. It must summarize what they would say were they speaking directly to the prospect. It must summarize facts and feelings that led them to first provide support.

The case for support is more than a working document. In the future it will chronicle the growth and development of an institution. It must use an official voice for it speaks for the whole institution.

The case for support should communicate effectively and personally. Therefore, the official voice must be peppered with quotations from current and past leaders who embody the spirit and values that provide the *raison d'etre* for this appeal.

Audience

The audience for the formal, written case is the major donor prospect, not the person in the street. Understand prior to writing who that prospect is in detail. What other charities does the prospect group support? Where is that prospect in life—age, family status, education, vocational development, etc. If an alumnus, what was the prospect involved in at school? If a parent, what, if any, special relationship does the individual have with the district? What is their child involved in at school, in the community?

Why be so concerned about such data? Because actions demonstrate what is important. People make the most generous gifts to the causes and institutions felt to be most important. In a busy world what is determined to be most important is as much a matter of shading as it is of substance.

The importance of the public school system is not what is at stake when writing the case for support. The question to be addressed is: What aspect and opportunity will meet a real need and provide the top prospect group with the most meaningful (important) opportunity to become involved? Such decisions go way beyond "creative packaging." They address an institution's and an individual's life values and reason for being. Where they match, large gifts result.

Length

One should be able to read and comprehend the basic facts within a 10-15 minute time period. Remember you are there to make a request that is easily understood.

The appropriate length of the print portion of the document increases with the quality of the design. Effective use of headlines, captions, and photos in combination with essential text can communicate a longer and more complex message while maintaining high readability. If forced by budget constraints to publish with basically a page of type, keep the case to no more than 2½ pages of loose type and rely on the use of headlines and box quotes to help the reader.

Tone

The tone of the case must be one of hope and opportunity placed on a base of success. Even the weakest system when measured against the standard yardsticks of post-high school performance contain examples of outstanding achievement. Begin with that achievement as the role model and build more of the same. Everyone has problems. Deal with them where solutions can be developed. This case must be the road map to implementing those solutions.

None of the above statements should be construed as a license to be less than truthful. To lie to your constituents is to drive them away for a generation and in all likelihood will destroy the foundation. The rule of thumb is—present a problem with a solution attached and the problem becomes an opportunity.

The following is a sample case statement prepared for the Montclair Foundation.

Draft case statement

The Montclair Foundation for Excellence in Education

"The Excellence Fund"

I Reasons for "The Excellence Fund"

The Excellence Fund seeks to provide the resources for that extra "margin of excellence" in educational programs. However, such an effort makes sense only because of the presence of a solid base of quality education upon which to build a structure of excellence—The Montclair Public Schools.

Montclair has always prided itself on its public schools. The challenge of educating all of the township's children is different from that of the surrounding areas. Montclair, far from being a typical New Jersey suburb, is, in the diversity of its population, much more like a small city. People of all races, creeds, national backgrounds, and aspirations live here. The job of its schools is to educate all of the children to become self-sustaining and contributing members of society.

Montclair citizens expect excellence in education. Most recently, Montclair's pioneering efforts have been directed toward establishing its magnet school program which allows parents to choose any school in the district for their child. The magnet school plan has not only successfully desegregated Montclair's schools but has also attracted residents from all over the county—because it is good education.

A number of elements in our school program are either highly unusual or unique to the township although residents already take them for granted: full day kindergarten; pre-school programs; transportation to any school in the district; gifted and talented education for all interested students; extended day programs; computer education, K-12; performing arts programs; advanced college placement courses; and a full and varied sports program.

While the rest of the nation is crying out for a back-to-basics education, clearly, in Montclair, parents are choosing Basics *Plus*. However, excellent education is expensive. And even in Montclair, where the willingness to provide public funds is traditional, existing resources can be stretched only so far. Yet there is still more to do!

State and federal grants helped finance much of the innovative programs described above. We have seen a shrinkage of that source of support. Therefore, we of the Montclair community must prepare to assume direct responsibility for financing continuing innovation and that extra edge of excellence that makes Montclair what it is!

II Goals of "The Excellence Fund"

- To help meet the needs of students for educational enrichment and to enable the district to provide learning opportunities that cannot be funded through normal revenue sources.
- To support innovation in the curriculum and in other programs sponsored by the public schools.
- To affirm and strengthen broad-based citizen involvement in public education.
- To encourage and reward exceptional leadership in faculty, staff and volunteers.

III The Special Role of "The Excellence Fund"

There is no thought that our efforts will replace tax dollars—that is not our purpose any more than the private school alumni fund replaces tuition. Our intent is, through cooperation with the Montclair Board of Education and administration, to develop annually projects for enriching public education: those that "*could* be" if extra dollars were available.

Likewise our intent is not to replicate nor shadow the work of the Board of Education. To the contrary, it is confidence in the work being done that makes consideration of an effort such as this possible. The goal will be to enhance the effectiveness of current governing bodies by developing additional support (both emotional and tangible in the form of programs or program dollars) from citizens of Montclair and the constituencies of The Montclair Public Schools.

IV Where did "The Excellence Fund" come from?

The real beginnings of "The Excellence Fund" lie within the very fabric and nature of the Montclair community. The public school system could not have met the challenges of the past decades without open leadership that led to an unusually high degree of productive citizen involvement in seeking and implementing effective solutions to local problems.

Personal commitment to meeting the diverse needs of our children has traditionally been a hallmark of individuals and organizations in Montclair. In that tradition, individuals have come together to form a Steering Committee of volunteer citizens seeking to establish a permanent vehicle to encourage and facilitate such personal involvements: The Montclair Foundation for Excellence in Education.

14 Managing a public relations program

by David P. Brown

Public relations is an integral part of any successful effort to develop awareness, recognition, and image. How an organization is perceived, and how well information about that organization is communicated, can be greatly influenced by a comprehensive public relations effort.

Public relations is a function of management. It is not merely ancillary to sales and marketing or personnel operations. Whereas it supports all areas of an organization, it should be a separate entity contributing to the overall objectives and philosophy of the organization and helping the organization adapt to its changing world.

Public relations practitioners have offered a variety of definitions for their profession from "helping an organization and its public accommodate each other" to the more elaborate "all activities and attitudes intended to judge, adjust to, influence, and direct the opinion of any group or groups of persons in the interest of any individual group or institution."

However defined, public relations must have certain qualities: professionalism, clear-cut objectives, organization, and consistent standards.

Educational institutions have a particular need for effective public relations. The widespread publics to which they must communicate and the necessary interaction with the community make the job of public relations for school systems difficult. However, effective public relations can play a significant role in the success of a public school system.

One definition, as put forth by Charles Steinberg in "The Creation of Consent: Public Relations in Practice," notes that public relations contributes to the "structuring of philosophy and carrying out of that philosophy in practice so that what the institution says is not at variance with what it does."

Before developing goals and procedures for a public relations program, the targets of your efforts, the various publics, must be considered. A school system has to communicate successfully with a number of groups or publics. These groups have different interests and thus require different strategies for effective communications.

The target groups, both within the school system and outside, include:

I. External
    A. Parents
    B. Companies, fraternal and civic groups
    C. Alumni
    D. Other institutions (churches, private and parochial schools, community service agencies, etc.)
    E. Community-at-large
    F. Government agencies
    G. Other educational organizations

II. Internal
    A. Teachers and staff
    B. Unions
    C. Students
    D. Boards.

With these target groups in mind, a worthy public relations program for a public school system could be established which would have among its goals:

1. Keeping the school's name and activities before the public in a favorable light.

2. Reinforcing the school's image as a leading institution in the community.

3. Communicating to a variety of publics (e.g., parents, teachers, alumni, business and civic leaders, the community-at-large) important information about the school and its operations.

4. Expanding awareness about the personnel, programs, and potential problems of the school system.

5. Developing a climate of receptivity for new programs, budget decisions, etc.

6. Maintaining a system to allow effective reaction to problems and negative publicity which could hamper operations.

7. Increasing morale of faculty, staff, and students, thus enhancing productivity and efficiency.

8. Fostering goodwill among the community, government agencies, local businesses, organizations, and institutions.

To achieve these objectives a four-part program of professional public relations is required:

I. Media relations

Does the school have a good rapport with local media? Is the preponderance of coverage about budgets and "bad news?" What should we do as an organization to enhance the kind of media attention we want? Are we overlooking possible "good news" stories? How can we develop systems to supply information to the media?

II. Community relations

Does the school really play an important role in the community? How do community leaders perceive us? What steps can be taken to increase cooperative efforts between businesses, civic organizations, and others? Whose responsibility is the school's relationship with the community?

III. Publications

What is the purpose of our publications and do they work? Do our publications reflect the same professionalism we expect from our faculty and staff? Are we wasting money on ineffective publications? Is our material being read and understood? How can our publications be best handled with existing staff?

IV. Internal communications

Do faculty and staff have an understanding of public relations objectives? Is there a clear line of communications between the board and the rest of the school system? How can morale be improved through public relations efforts?

Media relations

Being part of a well-read feature story, appearing favorably in the news columns, serving as a source for education trend articles and having your school's name discussed on television and radio are some results of good media relations.

Media relations can be divided into two segments: print and broadcast.

The print media can reach a cross-section of the population through a variety of approaches—the mass appeal of a daily newspaper, the individualized attraction of special newspaper sections (e.g., sports, business, arts and entertainment), general interest magazines, publications targeted at specific geographic (regional magazines, for example) or demographic readers (computer or fashion magazines), trade and professional journals.

With expanded news formats, public service possibilities,

and a variety of talk shows, radio and television are becoming increasingly effective in dissemination of information at the local and regional levels.

Knowing how to reach the media is important. This requires an awareness of the philosophy of the publication, the focus of various departments within the publication, and the criteria of decision making editors.

For example, the hiring of a grade school teacher may be of no interest to an editor of a major daily newspaper, but a small weekly that concentrates on your area might find it newsworthy. An innovative computer teaching program could appeal to an editor at a large newspaper, but certainly not the entertainment or sports editor.

Take time to learn about media in your area.

WHO...

. . .are the reporters covering schools and education, or the area in which your school is located?

. . .decides the content of various newspaper sections?

. . .is responsible for listings and calendars of events?

WHAT...

. . .should be included in press releases to different editors and news directors?

. . .is the focus of a particular radio talk show?

. . .is the best approach to interest television in a school project?

WHEN...

. . .are the deadlines for different information (sports scores, announcements of events)?

. . .are the publication dates for special sections (Back-to-School, Christmas)?

. . .is the best time of day to call? Reporters and editors have deadlines to meet and are not available at certain times of the day. Check before contacting them at those times.

WHERE...

. . .should information be sent?

. . . does the publication or radio station consider its coverage area?

. . . are the radio and television studios located?

Setting up a media relations program

It is crucial to have an on going, consistent effort in media relations. This requires a staff member who has the expertise and time to successfully plan and execute the program or it may require an assistant from outside professional services.

The program should include a long-term organizational plan with flexibility built in to accommodate unforeseen developments. Some crucial items to consider:

—Select the right person or persons to organize and execute the program.

—Make sure the individuals have sufficient time, support, and access to information; a person encumbered by too many other tasks cannot effectively handle a good media relations effort.

—Establish reasonable expectations.

—Develop a workable plan that includes basic news releases, feature story ideas, etc.

—Set deadlines for ideas to be discussed, for information to be gathered, for press releases to go out, for contacting media (e.g., don't wait until the day before to inform the press about an event).

—Encourage involvement through contribution of ideas and assistance in writing and distribution of press releases.

—Have contingency plans to deal with "bad news."

Community relations

By nature, schools are fully involved in community relations, from parent-teacher activities to student presentations and sports events. However, often no comprehensive plan exists to enhance the overall public relations effort through community projects.

A number of ways exist to work with existing programs to improve community relations and raise the visibility of the school and its accomplishments. For example, a science fair may be organized as a joint venture with a local high tech company, which could provide funding and expertise. In addition, certain exhibits may be put on display at the company or in locations around the community after the event at the school is over.

Joint ventures—shared activities with one or more organizations—are excellent for improving community relations and strengthening finances. Professional arts organizations, government agencies, companies, service groups and others will work with schools in developing projects that are good for the whole community. Through shared interests, staffing, and cross-pollination of ideas, joint ventures can benefit all involved.

Schools can maintain good community relations through speaking engagements with community groups. A speakers' bureau, in which faculty and staff are made available to civic organizations, church groups and others, can be very effective in nurturing goodwill. Teachers, staff, and students should be rewarded for their contributions in boosting community relations, thus encouraging further involvement.

Everyone in the school system should understand the community relations impact of individual and group actions, whether it is a one-on-one meeting with a parent or a number of volunteers helping at a hospital. Each activity affects the overall image of the school.

Community relations should be an action-oriented endeavor. In this perspective, some of the actions schools might consider are:

—Speakers' bureaus.

—Joint ventures with companies, institutions and organizations.

—Select student groups to represent the school.

—Allowing community groups to use school facilities.

—Encouragement of staff involvement with community-based organizations.

As Wilbur J. Peak, former Vice President for Public Relations of Illinois Bell Telephone Co., observed about community relations: "Act in regard to the community, think in terms of groups and address yourself to the individual."

Publications

The effective use of publications can play a major role in a school system's communications effort. Many areas are affected by a publication—media relations, community relations, internal communications.

Thus, the function, direction, and development of the publication must be clearly defined. The next chapter will examine the following points related to publications:

1. Steps in determining needs, direction, and function of a publication.

2. Developing format, content, design, frequency, and distribution.

3. How to produce quality publications (staffing, costs, deadlines, etc.).

4. Uses of various publications.

5. Ways of measuring publication effectiveness.

Internal communications

A thorough public relations program should also consider internal communications, (e.g., effectively reaching staff, the board of education, students).

Although the techniques for reaching the general public or community leaders may be different, the need for awareness and understanding is similar. Concern and effort to communicate internally should be as great as that for external public relations.

A plan for internal communications should be included in the overall public relations program . . . memos, publications, regular informational meetings, use of bulletin boards and public address systems

The lack of good internal communications can have a detrimental affect on the overall public relations program, through misunderstandings, misinformation, or apathy.

15 Organizing a publications program

Before designing specific documents one must first review where you are. Gather a number of individuals from all segments of the school district and the general community in a room. Have displayed a piece of every printed communication emanating from the district, from internal memos and purchase orders to report cards and newsletters. Give people time to review and handle the documents.

Next bring them around a table with the documents displayed in the center and ask them:

1. What do the documents or reports say?
2. To whom are they saying it?
3. How often should they be distributed?

List the responses on newsprint or chalk board.
The following list is the result of such an exercise.

Communication goals

What Do You Want To Say?	To Whom?	How Often?*
1. What is special about our school district?	prospective parents general community	once ongoing

What Do You Want To Say?	To Whom?	How Often?*
2. Who are our leading people?	prospective parents	once
	general community	ongoing
3. How is school relevant today?	in house family	ongoing
4. How does the district relate to other community resources?	prospective parents	once
	general community	ongoing
	parents	ongoing
5. Come to school.	prospective parents	once
	prospective students	once
6. What being a student's parent means.	prospective parents	once
	current parents	ongoing
7. Report student progress.	in house family	ongoing/ frequently
8. Describe current curriculum.	prospective parents	once
9. Discuss curriculum issues.	in house family	ongoing
10. Who is in the family?	current parents and students	ongoing
11. Who are the faculty?	prospective parents	once
	current family	ongoing
12. What are alumni doing?	full constituency	ongoing
13. Announce activities/events.	in house family	frequently
14. The school is well managed.	prospective donors	ongoing
	taxpayers	
15. Vision of the future.	donors	ongoing
	current parents	ongoing
	prospective parents	once
16. School needs—financial	in house and friends	ongoing
17. School needs—volunteer	in house and friends	ongoing
18. School needs—in kind gifts	in house and friends	ongoing
19. Class activities.	in house families	frequently
20. Parent counsel activities.	parents and faculty	ongoing/ frequently
21. What must I do to enroll?	prospective families	once
22. What must I do to register?	parents and students	ongoing
23. Who do I call for what?	in house family	ongoing
24. Who are the district's leaders?	in house family	ongoing

* *ongoing:* a publication dealing with issues that need repeated presentation. Issues may be discussed at length or in a publication containing information that changes little within a specific period of time.

frequently: a publication that contains brief articles dealing with issues that come and go rapidly, like announcing events.

once: a publication that has a long shelf life measured in years. It contains more universal information, rather than working data.

Organizational principles

Review the whole list, eliminating duplicates and adding any which the administration or faculty feel the volunteers may have overlooked. The next task is to distill the above list into a coordinated publications program. Creating a single publication is not an easy task, much less designing a program to fit the district and its constituents. One must consider the many audiences, messages, the content's timeliness, as well as the possible mediums and formats one could use.

I use a number of guiding principles when attempting such a synthesis:

Principle 1) Initially design each publication with as *few* separate messages and audiences as possible. Do not ask any one publication to be all things to all constituencies. (Some combining will become obvious later.)

Principle 2) Format responds to content, together they determine timeliness. (Do not attempt to publish weekly notices in a journal focusing on curriculum issues.)

Principle 3) Make each printing serve as many audiences as possible.

Principle 4) Provide only the content that each constituent needs.

Publication alternatives

New Family Packet

A review of the list of communication objectives regarding new residents reveals that all the new resident objectives were to be stated on a one time basis. This makes practical the presentation of all that material in a single package. Most of the material could also be prepared on a two to three year cycle rather than recreating the whole piece each year.

In general the material falls into two categories, broad district wide issues, and more specific individual school building concerns.

District View Book

> Message: This district is a productive place to grow.
> Content: General description of district
> 1. What is the history of the district?
> 2. Who are its notable people?
> 9. Describe the district's curriculum.
> Format: Publish on a three year cycle. Eleven by 8½", 8 to 12 pages plus cover; typeset with pictures.

Specific School Insert

> Message: This school can serve your child.
> Content: Specific description of a school's program
> 4. How does this school use the resources of the district and the community?
> 5. Come to this school.
> 6. What being a parent at this school means.
> 9. Describe the district's curriculum.
> Format: Publish on a three year cycle. Eleven by 8½", 8 to 12 pages, including cover; typeset with pictures.

Enrollment Supplement

> Message: How to enroll my child in the district.
> Content: Steps and forms necessary to enroll child.
> 22. What must I do to enroll?
> Format: Published every two years. Eight-and-a-half by 11", 4 pages, typeset; black and white, forms perforated for ease of use.

School Registration Supplement

> Message: How to register my child for classes, athletics, other extracurricular activities, etc.
> Content: Steps and forms necessary to register child for specific activities.
> 23. What must I do to register?
> Format: Published annually. Eight-and-a-half by 11″, 2 pages; typeset with insert.

Faculty Roster

> Message: Our faculty are high quality and accessible.
> Content: Photo with biographical information on teacher and description of duties. Should also be cross referenced by department/duties. Should include list of who to call for what.
> 11. Who are the school's faculty?
> Format: Published annually by school. Eight-and-a-half by 11″, 8 pages; typeset; booklet with photos if possible.

Complete the packet by including recent issues of the newsletter or bulletin. Also have a "New Family" envelope printed to hold the material. Then, distribute this packet through a welcome wagon, real estate dealers, corporate personnel offices and so on.

Annual report

The community has a responsibility to understand the trends and movements within the district they support. The district has a need to annually present its strengths and concerns to its constituents.

> Message: The school district is innovative and well managed.
> Content: A report of the actions of the school board and the foundation trustees, the institutional activities of the school, including budget summary, a report on giving to the school, an honor role of donors

and volunteers, and an appeal for the current year annual fund.

4. How does the district relate to other community resources?
14. The district is well managed.
15. Vision of the future.
16. School needs—financial.
20. Parent counsel activities.

Format: Eight-and-a-half by 11″, 8 pages plus cover; typeset with pictures; magazine format; self mailer; annual fund response envelope also included; published in the fall.

Distribution: Everyone in constituency, sent with cover letter to last year's donors and all parents asking that they give to the annual fund again.

Parent/student handbook

Upon close examination there is a significant body of information that needs to be available for reference by the parents and students. A great deal of that information stays the same from year to year making possible a two to three year handbook.

Message: Here is how to live happily in the district.
Content:

3. How is school relevant today?
6. What being a parent of a current student means.
9. Describe current curriculum (import from new family packet).
13. Announce annual activities, events (school calendar).
20. Class activities (describe).
23. What must I do to register (import from new family packet)?

Format: A two year publication with a second year update insert. Size and production specifications to be defined.

Distribution: Given to new parents at opening of school and to all parents after two year update.

Community roster

There is a significant collection of information that must be revised each year such as class rosters, new addresses, annual calendar, current lab fees, and a wide range of other issues. Such information falls naturally as part of the community roster as well as the basic communication information outlined below.

> Message: Here is the school family
> Content: The information necessary for effective communication within the school family. Include: student roster by class with phone numbers, cross referenced with a family roster with full family names, addresses, and phones. Also include leadership lists with phone numbers. The center section would be the faculty roster printed for the new family packet, including the listing of "Who to call for what...."
> 10. Who is in the family?
> 11. Who are the faculty?
> 23. Who to call for what?
> 24. Who are the district's leaders?
> Format: Eleven by 8½", 8 to 12 pages; typewriter set; booklet.
> Distribution: To all families at the opening of school.

School bulletin

Announcing class trips, final due dates for library books, exam schedules, and so forth all need communicating in a timely and readable way. Such information is best packaged in small articles of one to two paragraphs. The logical vehicle is a "Quick notes" format.

> Message: Daily living information—who is doing what, and what do I have to do in response, or to make it possible...."
> Content:
> 8. Report student progress.
> 14. Announce activities/events.

18. School needs—volunteer.
19. School needs—in kind gifts.
20. Class activities.
Format: Eight-and-a-half by 11″ folded to a number 10 size self mailer; preprinted 2 color mast head; typewriter set; photo copied or printed off set.
Distribution: Weekly, hand carried home by the students, mailed to a select list of community leaders and/or donor prospects.

School newsletter

Some issues need more room to develop for people to understand. New programs need explaining as does dropping old ones. Student and faculty achievements often warrant more than a paragraph announcement. The idea vehicle for such articles in the newsletter. It allows further development of issues yet is published frequently enough to respond to timely issues.

Message: The district family lives, works, and succeeds.
Content: Twenty-five percent faculty/curriculum issues or profile; 25 percent student/alumni activity stories, 25 percent promotion or explanation of activities, 25 percent general house keeping, monthly calendar, accounts of actions taken.
3. How is school relevant today?
6. What being the parent of a student means.
7. Report student progress.
8. Describe current curriculum.
12. What are alumni doing?
13. Announce activities and events.
14. The school is well managed.
15. Vision of the future.
16. to 18. School needs—financial, volunteer, gifts in kind.
20. Parent counsel activities.
Format: Eight-and-a-half by 11″, 4 to 6 pages; two color mast head; folds to a 5½″ by 8½″ self mailer.
Distribution: Monthly, August to June.

Faculty Journal

In the end the quality of a school district lies with the faculty. Success breeds success. Establish a forum to showcase the work of those who implement the programs of excellence we all hope for.

> Message: Our faculty and our alumni contain leaders in their fields.
>
> Content: A forum for the presentation of faculty/student/parent scholarly or artistic work, and the discussion of broader curriculum or institutional issues.
>
> 1. What is special about our school district?
> 3. How is school relevant today?
> 4. How does the district relate to and employ other community resources?
> 6. What being the parent of a student means.
> 9. Discuss curriculum issues.
> 12. What are alumni doing?
> 15. Vision of the future.
>
> Format: Eight-and-a-half by 11", 8 to 12 pages, magazine format with cover; limited pictures.
>
> Distribution: Once or twice each year mailed to whole constituency.

16   Managing district events

A commitment to excellence means a commitment to involvement. No area illustrates this better than special events. The numerous functions that are sponsored by the superintendent, the building principals, the yet-to-be-developed alumni association, the fathers' association, mothers' association and foundation development office, all provide countless opportunities for volunteers and staff to involve everyone in the preservation and development of a stronger community through education.

This chapter provides some action checklists in outline form to prompt thinking about facilitating involvement. It is basically a "how to" guide or manual on the planning of events through an office of external affairs. Establishing such a support office within the district, or within the foundation as a service to the district, permits the coordination of a focused events program. Each event depends on the dedication of people who are willing to devote enough time and energy to make them successful. The goal of this manual is to make the volunteer's work easier.

Events coordinator

An events coordinator has two roles: 1) To provide special opportunities for developing community pride and involvement within the programs of the district and 2) to work with the volunteer and staff leadership of district events to extend the event's benefits through a greater involvement of a broader base of individuals. Such an extension will maximize each event's potential as a showcase of the excellence within the programs of the district.

Events coordinator responsibilities

1. To plan, coordinate, and implement all details necessary for the successful execution of the foundation, and foundation-related events managed through an office of external affairs. These events will range from board or committee meetings involving coffee for several people to a full dinner for 200 or more.

2. To administer all such activities using established district or foundation policies and procedures, and maintain all records, files, and information associated with each event.

3. To act as a liaison between the foundation and all related departments, associations, and individuals in regard to events jointly sponsored by the foundation and any of their constituencies. Specifically, it is the function of the events coordinator to coordinate and direct the flow of information (e.g. work requests, meeting memos, purchasing, billing).

Another key function of an events coordinator is to establish the dates and times for events. Determine dates early to avoid interference with the schedules of athletic teams, academic and extracurricular activities, special tests, field trips, workshops, concerts, plays, and all holidays.

The difficulty of this task is increased because many parents have children enrolled in several district schools. Each has its own extensive calendar of events. Here are the steps the events coordinator should follow when scheduling events.

1. Prior to the end of the school year, usually in late May or early June, the events coordinator should schedule a meeting to tentatively establish event dates and times for the upcoming school year. Usually, school year events will fall roughly around the same dates of the previous school year's events. This meeting should include the following people or their representatives:
   a. Director of foundation
   b. Superintendent
   c. Events coordinator
   d. Parent organization leaders
   e. Booster club leaders
   f. Alumni association pres.
   g. Building principals
   h. Other administrative staff with dean of student-type responsibilities.

2. During the meeting, it should be made clear exactly what events, if any, are to be excluded, and what events are to be added to the new calendar.

3. Following the meeting, the events coordinator should construct a rough draft of the new calendar. The draft must include all events and meetings managed through the foundation office, as well as all other district events.

4. Once the new events calendar rough draft has been constructed, copies should be distributed to all people mentioned above, with a cover letter asking for any corrections by a specific date.

5. The calendar should then be adjusted accordingly with any incoming corrections.

6. Scheduling conflicts should be resolved by the events coordinator through letters, memos,

phone calls, or meetings with the appropriate department head(s) and the appropriate volunteer(s). In doing so, the events coordinator should keep the superintendent, director of the foundation and the building principals informed as to the nature and progress of all conflicts and resolutions.

7. Following the rough draft construction of the new events calendar and the resolution of all scheduling conflicts, the events coordinator should obtain a copy of the official building and district calendars. All calendars should then be checked against each other for any further conflicts.

8. At this point, any additional calendar conflicts should be noted by the events coordinator and turned over to the superintendent and foundation director for final resolution.

9. Once all conflicts have been resolved and the events coordinator has all necessary dates and times, a final draft of the new events calendar should be constructed.

10. Copies of the new events calendar should be distributed to everyone involved.

Proper scheduling will make or break an events coordinator. No other area of an events coordinator's job is more critical to the successful management of events.

Scheduling an event, like launching a spacecraft, requires a systematic approach. Prepare for events long before they actually occur in descending order of difficulty and length of time. The countdown is as follows:

1. *Systems check—the summer months . . .*
   The summer is the best time to plan for all upcoming school year events. Along with the scheduling process, the following should be tackled during the summer:

a. Events calendar

b. Event checklists

c. Event accounting forms

d. Filing

e. Entire year's work requests for all associations and foundation meetings and events

f. List of events requiring foundation staff or volunteer attendance (distributed to staff and volunteer leadership)

g. List of all event sites (distributed to maintenance and all department heads affected by event venue)

2. *Eight weeks prior to event and counting...*

   Contact all outside clubs or facilities where an event might occur. Secure bids, decide upon the location, have it approved by the appropriate volunteer and staff, and then commit to event date and time.

3. *Six weeks...*

   a. Make all special planning purchases and rentals requiring this much advance planning

   b. Notify all appropriate persons of upcoming pre-event planning meetings (usually in writing)

   c. Confirm menus and prices with outside facilities

   d. Notify mailing house of upcoming bulk mailing

   e. Notify printer of upcoming printing needs

4. *Five weeks...*

   a. Have invitations printed

   b. Obtain invitation list

   c. Process purchase order for bulk mailing and postage

   d. Deliver bulk mailing materials to mailing house

5. *Four weeks . . .*

   a. Mail invitations and fliers announcing event

   b. Contact caterer, secure bids if necessary, commit to date, time, and location

   c. Hold pre-event planning meetings with appropriate people

   d. Secure entertainment for event

   e. Arrange for event volunteers

   f. Secure any special prizes or awards needed for presentation at event

6. *Three weeks . . .*

   a. Arrange with building dining room for event's food needs

   b. Set and confirm menu with caterer or outside facility

7. *Two weeks . . .*

   a. Make all necessary purchases and rentals for event (see *Purchasing*)

   b. Send reminder memo to anyone whose program will be affected by the event

   c. Deliver program to printer

   d. Walk through event location—Anticipate what could go wrong!

8. *One week . . .*

   a. R.S.V.P. deadline—deliver event attendance list (should be set up and kept updated) to appropriate persons

   b. Process work request and deliver to appropriate personnel, including maintenance, dining rooms and other site supervisors (see *Work request*)

    c. Do all minor art work, signs, maps needed for event

9. *Day of event. . .*

    a. Check the event site with the work request in hand and make sure everything is there and in its proper place

    b. ATTEND IT (either the events coordinator or a member of the foundation staff, depending upon the preestablished attendance schedule)

    c. Note what did and did not work, recording comments and suggestions for the post-event evaluation

    d. Make sure arrangements have been made for the clean-up and collection of any unused materials

10. *One day to one week after event. . .*

    a. Make arrangements to have all rented equipment returned

    b. Have the post-event evaluation filled out by all who were involved with the planning of the event as well as those who worked

    c. Compile a post-event report which should include all post-event evaluations and the event accounting form. Distribute the report to those involved in planning and execution of the event

    d. If needed, schedule a post-event meeting. Include all who were involved with the planning of the event. Review problems and note recommendations for the next year's program.

Naturally, all of the above details will not apply to every event. Those that do apply, however, should be scheduled on a *specific day* and checked off as the task is completed. The following pointers may help the events coordinator with the scheduling process.

188 | MANAGING DISTRICT EVENTS

1. Use a weekly desk pad calendar. Because of the many details the events coordinator may have to attend to on any given day, a monthly desk pad calendar is not practical. It is also helpful to have the entire week's agenda visible at a glance.

2. Allow at least a three day leeway when scheduling details. The events coordinator can always expect attending to details he/she did not count on. If a detail is scheduled three days before its deadline, rushing may be avoided.

3. Use a "tickler," which is no laughing matter. It could save the events coordinator a headache. A tickler is a small note placed on the desk pad calendar a few days before a deadline reminding the events coordinator of an upcoming task.

Beyond a doubt, filing remains the key to organization in any office system. Another important function of the events coordinator is to keep accurate records—poor records only cause more work. The following events filing system allows for smooth yearly transfer and consolidation of the enormous amounts of event details that must be accounted for. Regardless of how many events planned, there will always be a need to examine procedures used the previous year(s). If used properly, the following system will provide reliable information at the most pertinent times—when you need it!

After the events calendar has been established for the upcoming school year, new files for events must be created. Although each individual may have his or her own system of filing, every major event file should contain a folder for each of the four major components that are involved with event planning. They are:

a. Work requests and purchase orders

b. Food and beverage arrangements

c. Correspondence

d. Printed materials.

The events coordinator should realize that a system is not a system unless it is consistently used.

The new files for events should be organized in chronological order using Pendaflex hanging folders, with each event category having its own color code, for example:

    a. WHITE—School events

    b. YELLOW—Alumni association events

    c. RED—Mothers' association events

    d. GREEN—Fathers' association events.

At this point during the filing process, complete event checklists for the new event files using information found on the event checklist in the corresponding event file of the past academic or fiscal year. A sample checklist is included in this chapter.

After completing and filing new event checklists, establish new event accounting forms with all available information, such as the event name, time, location, account number, and the new budgets of each event. File the event accounting form with the event checklist in an event file.

Following the construction of the new files, the event checklists, and event accounting forms, integrate the past academic or fiscal year files into an events history file, which is organized alphabetically under the appropriate school or external association heading.

Adjust the events history file directory according to all new information filed within the events history file.

Event budgets

During January, the events coordinator projects all event budget amounts for the following academic or fiscal year. Projections are based upon the costs of programming events during the present year and previous years, recommendations made in post-event evaluations, and an estimation of a market price increase.

Once the event budget projections have been established, they are sent to the proper authorities for final approval.

The events coordinator should expect the final event budgets in May. Take these budgets seriously or lose one of the major benefits to maintaining an events coordinator—cost effective management. It is the event coordinator's responsibility to remain within budgets when planning for events for the upcoming year.

Purchasing

In most events, planning will require a certain amount of purchasing, whether it be equipment rental, payment for services, or outright acquisition. Regardless of the type of purchase, each must be made using standard district or foundation procedures. Below is a description of a possible system:

1. Event budget (see also *Event budgets)*—will determine how much purchasing may be done on any given event. The events coordinator must stay within the allotted budget.

2. Events coordinator—is responsible for all event purchasing for events assigned to it for management.

3. The event checklist will guide the events coordinator as to the purchasing needs for an event.

4. Supplier bids—should be obtained by the events coordinator from all potential service/wholesale/retail organizations. The events coordinator should periodically canvass suppliers to ensure the most competitive prices and the best values.

5. The volunteer leadership must approve all purchases recommended by the events coordinator.

6. Item/service order—should be made by the events coordinator based upon the appropriate approval.

7. Appropriate purchase orders must be completed by the events coordinator for all event purchases.

8. The appropriate portion of the purchase order should be filed in the appropriate event file.

9. The school purchasing agent should receive copies of all event purchase orders to facilitate delivery of goods and services and payment of bills.

Billing

With the quantity of purchasing the events coordinator must do throughout the school year, he or she will invariably need to administer a certain amount of billing paperwork. Normally, any service/retail/wholesale organization will bill directly to a designated business office. Although this process is effective in terms of the organization receiving payment, it precludes the events coordinator from ensuring that the event got what was paid for since he or she arranged for the purchase. For this reason, the events coordinator should request that a duplicate bill be sent to his or her attention.

Work requests

All institutions have an internal structure for assigning work. The maintenance and food service staff, under the direction of the business manager within the district, must satisfy the work requests of the superintendent, the administrators, the faculty and staff members, and all external associations while meeting the daily needs of all district facilities and hundreds of students. With this amount of responsibility, it would be nearly impossible to accomplish even a portion of the workload without an efficient, manageable system.

The key to working within such a system is the use of standard work request forms. Any time the maintenance or food service staff is needed to perform a task, no matter how small, a written work request must be completed. Perhaps more than any other district employee, the events coordinator must realize that proper use of the work request system is vital to the successful execution of his or her job responsibilities.

The following is a summary of the work request system along with some samples of actual event information/checklists and work request forms.

1. Past years' event information/checklist—helps the events coordinator establish the needs, based on past events needs, of the maintenance and food service staff for the upcoming events.

2. Events coordinator completes all event work requests.

3. Pre-event planning meeting (if necessary)—is held to identify all needs for an event.

4. Proper completion of the event checklist identifies all needs of the maintenance and food service staff.

5. Rough draft event work request providing preliminary outline of all needs of the maintenance and food service staff for each upcoming event shared with all principals involved with the event.

6. Final draft of event work request—should be completed by the events coordinator after all corrections have been made.

7. File copy—a file copy of the work request should be filed in the appropriate event file.

8. Key building supervisors should receive a copy of the work request.

EVENT PLANNING

CHANGE OF EVENT NOTICE

Events: *Any Event*

Publications: ——

Other: ——

ADDITION TO CALENDAR: ——

DELETION FROM CALENDAR: ——

CHANGED TO: *Date - 10/5/85*

CHANGED FROM: *Date - 10/4/85*

TO: Receptionist
     Barbara Speckhardt
     Business Office
     Maintenance
     Buttery
     Father's Association
     Mother's Association
     Alumni Association
     Other:

Signed: *Events Coordinator*

Date: *9/21/85*

ALUMNI / DEVELOPMENT
EVENT ACCOUNTING FORM

Event __*ANY*__   Date __10/5/85__   Sponsoring Association __*ALUMNI*__

Budget Account # __123.1__   Amount Allocated for Event __$ 500.00__

DATE	PURCHASE ORDER #	ITEM	AMOUNT	TOTAL SPENT-TO-DATE	EVENT BUDGET BALANCE-TO-DATE
					$ 500.00
9/15/85	5678	FOOD	$ 326.25	$ 326.25	173.75
9/22/85	9101	FLOWERS	53.17	379.42	120.58
9/25/85	1213	DECORATIONS	14.33	393.75	106.25
10/3/85	1415	BEVERAGES	65.28	459.03	40.97
10/5/85	1617	BARTENDER	40.00	499.03	.97
/ /					
/ /					
/ /					
/ /					
/ /					

Total Amount Spent $ 499.03

- -

EVENT BUDGET SUMMARY

AMOUNT ALLOCATED FOR EVENT $ 500.00   TOTAL CREDIT $ 787.29

+ CASH INTAKE FROM EVENT   287.29   TOTAL AMOUNT SPENT   499.03

TOTAL CREDIT $ 787.29   EVENT SURPLUS / DEFICIT $ 288.26

THE ALBANY ACADEMY

Academy Road   Albany, New York 12208
518-465-1461

PURCHASE ORDER *1234*

OUR P.O NUMBER **MUST** BE ON
INVOICE AND OUTSIDE CARTON

TAX EXEMPT
FORMS ON FILE
EX 100306

ALL DELIVERIES
Receiving Room
Hackett Blvd.

XYZ RENTAL
1002 CENTRAL AVE
ALBANY NY 12206

Date 9/21/85

OUR ACCOUNT NO. 123.4

QUANTITY	ITEM		TOTAL
100	FOLDING CHAIRS	@ .65	# 65.00
	DELIVERY	@ 20.00	20.00
		TOTAL	# 85.00

VENDOR

DIRECTOR OF ALUMNI / DEVELOPMENT
PURCHASING DEPT. PROGRAMS

THE ALBANY ACADEMY

INTERNAL WORK REQUEST

To: ☑ Buttery   Date: _9/30/85_

☑ Maintenance

Description in Detail:

Number of People _250_

Room Number(s) _BUTTERY_

Seating Required _250_

Date of Function _10/5/85_

Time: From _5:00_ To _7:00 PM_

Entrance(s) Required _MAIN AND SOUTH_

Other: _PLEASE HAVE THE FOLLOWING TO BUTTERY
BY 4:00 PM ON 10/5/85 :_

- 3 - 8' TABLES   • COFFEE/CREAM/SUGAR (150)
- 1 - CARD TABLE   • ACADEMY NAPKINS
- 100 - FOLDING CHAIRS   • ATTACHED BEVERAGE ORDER
- 3 WASTE BASKETS   • SEE EXTENDED WORK REQ.

Alumni / Development   DIRECTOR OF Alumni/
DEVELOPMENT PROGRAMS
Department Requesting   Authorized Signature

White: Business office   Canary: Buttery/Maintenance   Pink: File

ALBANY ACADEMY
ALUMNI/DEVELOPMENT OFFICE
EVENT CHECKLIST

Event _ANY EVENT_ Date _10/5/85_ Time _5:00-7:00 pm._

Location _BUTTERY_ Sponsoring Association _ALUMNI_

Estimated Attendance _250_

PRELIMINARIES. . . . .

☒ PRE-EVENT MEETING(S):

Date _9/21/85_

To attend:
__ Alumni/Development Director
__ Faculty
__ Business Manager
__ Staff
__ Buttery Head
☒ Alumni Assoc. Rep. _JOHN SMITH_
__ Maintenance Dept. Head
__ Father's Assoc. Rep. _____
__ Headmaster
__ Mother's Assoc. Rep. _____
☒ Events Coordinator
__ other _____

☒ ACADEMY FACILITIES:

__ Art Gallery
☒ Buttery
__ Chapel
__ Class Room _____
__ Field House
__ Headmaster's House/Yard
__ Library
__ Rest Room(s)
__ Student Lounge
__ Track
__ Trustee's Room
__ other _____

☒ MAP:

☒ Buttery
__ Library
__ Academy Grounds
__ Field House
__ Headmaster's house/yard
__ other _____

☒ WORK REQUEST:

To Business Office _9/30/85_

☒ EXTENDED WORK REQUEST:

To Business Office _9/30/85_

☐ RAIN PLAN

☒ OUTSIDE FACILITIES/CATERER:

Location/ Caterer _XYZ CATERING_

Contact _JIM_ Phone # _555-1212_

Guest List/Seating Chart delivered _/ /_

Menu arranged _9/23/85_

Prices set _9/23/85_

Final head count given _10/1/85_

PRINTING. . . . .

☒ INVITATIONS:

Drafted _9/1/85_

To be Approved by:
☒ Alumni/Development Director
☒ other _Alumni Rep._

To printer _9/2/85_

Back from printer _9/4/85_

Mailed _9/5/85_

☒ R.S.V.P./REGRETS:

Deadline _10/1/85_

Printout to:
☒ Alumni/Development Director
☒ Headmaster
☒ Other _Alumni Rep._

☐ GUEST LIST:

Obtained from _____

By _/ /_

☐ PROGRAM:

Drafted _/ /_

To be approved by:
__ Alumni/Development Director
__ Headmaster
__ Other _____

To printer _/ /_

Back from printer _/ /_

☐ POSTAGE:

P.O. to Business Office _/ /_

Check picked up _/ /_

Delivery to mailhouse _/ /_

☐ OFF-SET LETTER(S) MAILING:

To _____

RE: _____

Drafted _/ /_

To be approved by:
__ Alumni/Development Director
__ Headmaster
__ Other _____

To printer _/ /_

Back from printer _/ /_

Mailed _/ /_

To mailhouse _/ /_

FURNISHINGS. . . . .

[X] SCHOOL EQUIPMENT:

3 8' tables
___ 6' tables
1 card tables
20 buttery tables
___ Trustee table
___ Library tables
100 folding chairs
___ Trustee's chairs
___ ashtrays
[X] cash box(s)
[X] banner(s)
___ wastebasket(s)
[X] red plastic table cloth
___ white plastic table cloth
___ blackboard, eraser & chalk
[X] bar
___ other _____

1 trash cans/barrels
___ extension cord(s)
___ coat rack
___ p.a. system
___ risers
___ podium
___ screen
___ projector
___ easel(s)

[X] RENTED EQUIPMENT:

100 chairs
___ tables
___ tent
___ candleholders
___ phones
___ plants
___ other _____

[X] PURCHASES:

X flowers
[X] petty cash $ *30*
___ ad space
___ printing
___ decorations
___ candles
___ mailing services
___ postage
___ maintenance overtime
___ buttery overtime
___ other _____
_____
_____

DINNER & DRINKS. . . . .

[X] RECEPTION/DINNER:

Location ____*BUTTERY*____

Supplies:	Academy	Supplier: Caterer
X coffee for *150*	X	
___ tea	___	___
___ orange juice	___	___
___ tomato juice	___	___
X cream	X	___
X sugar	X	___
___ lemon	___	___
___ milk	___	___
___ chocolate milk	___	___
___ flowers	___	___
___ food	___	___
X linens	___	X
___ candles	___	___
___ paper plates	___	___
___ dolies	___	___
___ napkins	___	___
X Academy napkins	X	___
X eating utensils	___	X
___ condiments	___	___
X china	___	X
___ glasses	___	___
___ trays	___	___
___ push carts	___	___
___ Father's Assoc. warmers	X	___
___ Mother's Assoc. silver	X	___
[ ] spoons		
[ ] candleabras		
[ ] coffee/tea set		
[ ] punch bowls/ladles		
[ ] trays		
___ Mother's Assoc. linens	X	
___ punch	___	___
___ iced tea	___	___
___ plastic silverware	___	___
___ table numbers	___	___
___ podium	X	___
___ p.a. system	X	___
X wine	X	___

[ ] SEATING CHART:

To be approved by:
___ Alumni/Development Director
___ Headmaster
___ other _____

[ ] PLACE CARDS:

completed ___ / / ___

[X] BAR/SUPPLIES:

	Academy	Supplies: Cat.
X swizel sticks	X	
___ napkins		
___ Academy napkins	X	
X ice	___	___
___ block ice		
X ice chest(s)		
___ cork screw		
X ash trays	X	
___ wastebasket(s)		
___ cutting board w/knive		
___ pitchers		
___ can opener		
___ 7 oz. cups		
X 10 oz. cups		
___ styrofoam cups		
X tonic water	X	
X club soda		
X orange juice	X	
X bloody mary mix	X	
___ water		
X soda	X	
___ cannister soda		
___ soda machine (boosters)	X	
X liquor	X	
X beer	X	
X lemons		
X limes		
___ celery		
X bartender(s)		
___ other _____	___	

[X] DECORATIONS:

___ table decorations _____
___ plants
X directional signs "*DRINKS*"
___ flowers
___ posters _____
___ easel(s) _____
___ other _____

[ ] MUSIC/ENTERTAINMENT:

___ stereo/sound system
___ piano
___ other

PEOPLE/PARTICULARS. . . . .

☒ PEOPLE NEEDED:

___ student volunteer(s)
___ Father's Assoc. Volunteer(s)
___ Mother's Assoc. Volunteer(s)
☒ Alumni Assoc. Volunteer(s)
___ Administrator(s)
___ Faculty
___ Staff
☒ Alumni/Development Staff
___ Maintenance
☒ Buttery
___ other _____

☐ ACCOMMODATIONS:

___ list of available area accommodations
___ transportation needed
___ fruit, flowers, books, liquor, etc.
___ provided in special rooms
arrangements made ___ / /

☒ MISCELLANEOUS:

___ front row(s) reservations for V.I.P.'s
___ special parking arrangements
___ gift for speaker/V.I.P.
___ tape recorder
___ archives open
___ archives special display
___ photographs
☒ gavel
___ other _____

☒ REGISTRATION TABLE/SUPPLIES:

/ table(s) _6_ ft.
2 chair(s)
☒ sign(s) *"REGISTRATION"*
☒ pads/pencils/pens
☒ cash box
___ programs/literature
☒ volunteer list/schedule
___ sign-in register
☒ name tags
___ other _____

☐ POSTERS/SIGNS:

Description _____

Drafted __ / /

Posted __ / /

☐ PRIZES/AWARDS:

___ Academy picture
___ plaque
___ loving cup
___ Wendell
___ other _____

FURTHER DETAILS. . . . .

☒ CORRESPONDENCES:

Letters to: Re:

ACADEMY ALUMNI   *INVITATION*
_____   _____
_____   _____
_____   _____
_____   _____
_____   _____

Memos to: Re:

_____   _____
_____   _____
_____   _____
_____   _____
_____   _____

☒ POST-EVENT DETAILS:

☒ evaluation *10/7/85*

copies to:
☒ Alumni/Development Director
☒ Headmaster
___ other _____

☒ Event Accounting Form

☒ liquor count *10/5/85*

___ thank you's to:

_____
_____
_____
_____

☒ collect unused materials

☒ return equipment

___ clean up

☒ NOTES: *GOOD EVENT IN PAST -- STAY ON TOP OF EVERYTHING!*

ALBANY ACADEMY
ALUMNI/DEVELOPMENT OFFICE
POST EVENT EVALUATION

Event _ANY EVENT_   Date _10/5/85_   Time _5:00 - 7:00p.m._

Location _BUTTERY_   Sponsoring Association _ALUMNI_

Approximated Attendance _250_

RATING SCALE

GOOD: Planned Area needs no improvement.
ADEQUATE: Planned Area is sufficient, but could use upgrading.
INSUFFICIENT: Planned Area must be reformed incorporating Area "Comments/Recommendations."
N/A: Not Applicable

PLANNED AREA:	GOOD	ADEQUATE	INSUFFICIENT	N/A	COMMENTS/ RECOMMENDATIONS
Date & Time:	X				
Location:	X				
Pre-Event Communications:			X		MEET WITH MAINTENANCE BEFORE EVENT
Printing: (invitations, program, letter, etc.)					
Equipment:			X		NEED APPROX. 50 MORE CHAIRS
Food: (caterer, buttery)	X				GREAT!
Atmosphere: (decorations)		X			CONGESTED NEAR ENTRANCE
Volunteer Participation:	X				
Administrative Details: (work requests, memo's)	X				
Event Budget/Accounting:	X				
Other Services: (list)					

Further Comments: _____
GOOD EVENT -- PEOPLE STAYED TILL 9:00PM!

Completed by: _EVENTS COORDINATOR_   Date: _10/6/85_

17   Phonathons— A means to an end

Phonathons will raise dollars and in some instances large dollars. Moreover, a well-run phonathon will have a far reaching effect, way beyond the dollars raised.

What phonathons do well

1. Expand the base of support. Because success in phonathons is predicated on making a large number of calls, one obvious role for phonathons within a complete development program is that of expanding the base. Phonathons should be considered one of the early programs to implement; no other program of personal contact can do the same thing. In a more mature program, phonathons generally are not the prime solicitation method. They are used more as a clean up program.

2. Inform and solicit the uninitiated. Because in phonathons people speak directly with people, they provide an ideal program for influencing people. Mail contacts alone are easily ignored. A phone call, preceded and followed by an effective series of mail contacts, will have lasting educational impact and generate far more gifts.

3. Involve a large number of new workers. Although a

phone call provides a personal donor contact, for the solicitor it is still a relative anonymous procedure. In the early stages of the foundation many solicitors will think the foundation is a good idea, but they may be reluctant to make a personal visit. A phonathon will provide an excellent and non-threatening program for that first solicitation involvement.

4. *Solicit the initial gift.* Giving is in great part patterned behavior. The problem is getting the prospect to make that first gift. If the identity of the large donor was certain, it would make sense to invest the necessary institutional resources to secure that first gift, no matter how costly the solicitation. Since the identity of tomorrow's large donor is unknown, a cost effective way must be found to solicit many first time donors. Phonathons provide a perfect vehicle.

5. *Solicit the small and reluctant gift each year.* For donors who give less than $100, a phonathon provides an equally effective method of solicitation. This is especially true for prospects who have not responded to less personal methods, such as direct mail.

6. *Get information.* When properly managed, the foundation will receive a great deal of information from the phonathon. First, it will update donor addresses and phone numbers. If someone has moved in the past year, assume that something important has happened in that individual's life—marriage, divorce, birth of a child, job change, retirement. These events generally prompt a move and can affect the person's giving potential.

What phonathons do not do well

1. *Increase the average gift.* Increasing gift income, and hence the average gift, from the same donor base can be done most effectively by increasing the dollars contributed by the top donors. Although this may seem unfair to those

who are already giving the most, generally they can best afford such gifts.

Because substantial increases are best secured through a personal face-to-face call, it is more cost effective to focus on the larger donor, for costs to persuade an individual to increase their gift by 25 percent are the same whether that individual is giving $25 or $2500

2. *Solicit the larger gift.* To secure a large gift the prospect must be brought to a level of greater confidence in the investment. Thus, take greater time and effort to answer questions and explain the opportunity open to the prospective donor. That can only be done effectively through increased personal contact and a face-to-face encounter.

3. *Provide in depth information.* Phonathons are successful based on the number of calls completed. Although callers are to be encouraged to be personal and responsive with the people they call, they must keep moving. Therefore, avoid in depth conversations.

Two models — volunteer or paid callers

One can operate successful phonathons employing either volunteers or paid callers. Consider both alternatives. I prefer volunteers.

1. *Volunteers build* esprit de corps. A case can be made that the paid callers are more cost effective because they tend to secure a larger average gift and complete more calls. However, an equally strong case can be made that the residual of ownership in the volunteers, the affirmation of classmates calling classmates, more than makes up for the fewer dollars.

2. *Paid callers provide more effective solicitation.* Because the workers are paid demands can be more, such as extensive training and greater attention to detail. In addition, it is possible to give paid workers poorer prospects without increasing their frustration and running the risk of potentially turning them off to future work.

Goal setting

1. Define program and dollar goals. A phonathon will do little more than raise dollars unless goals are clearly defined and plans are in place to make them happen. What do you want to say to the prospect about the foundation in addition to its need for money? What do you want to learn about your donor's attitudes or goals? Perhaps include a small questionnaire to be used during each call. Prepare sample statements for your callers.

2. Determine dollar potential. Two factors will determine the success of your phonathon—the quality of the prospect list and the total number of hours of phoning. One volunteer working steadily for two hours should generate 15-20 gifts. Because this is a new venture with no past donors, that average could be somewhat lower. Likewise, the average gift will be somewhat below what you can expect in future years. A strong average gift in the first year would be in the range at $20–$30. If employing 15 callers per night for four nights, set a goal in the range of $15,000–$20,000. Such an effort would require beginning with 900-1,200 prospects.

Identifying prospects to be solicited

1. What list can you develop? There will be a tendency for well-meaning volunteers and staff to acquire lists of donors from other institutions, such as local theatre groups or clubs. These lists will be valuable but not as prospect lists. Prospect lists must come from within the programs of the district. Because people give to another cause does not mean they are a prospect for your cause.

You already have lists that will be of value for prospects: former school board members, leadership and members of the parent organizations, parents of the top 10 percent of the student body, alumni singled out at the time of graduation for special honors, past football players, parents of current students who play sports, or classroom volunteers.

It will take more work to develop the lists yourselves, but the prospect list will be better because it will be composed of those who already have or potentially have a relationship with the public schools. The foundation can build on the list during solicitation. Also, further information is available on the individuals.

2. *How much information can you get on each prospect?* The more known the more personal and meaningful is the solicitation. When doing research on prospects, these lists can be invaluable. In chapter 11 one can find a full discussion of what information to look for. At a minimum seek:

   a. home address

   b. phone number

   c. relationship to the district: alumnus, parent, local business owner

   d. past volunteer activity within the district

   e. past community service.

Enlisting your workers

1. *Who makes an effective caller?* Effective workers can come from any sector of the community. The important characteristic for a caller to possess is the abililty to distinguish between someone unwilling to give to the cause and personal rejection. Secondly, workers must be diligent. The number of calls made is the key to success. The more quiet, persistent individual often makes the best caller.

2. *Conducting an enlistment phonathon.* The most efficient enlistment process is a mailing sent to likely prospects followed up by a phone call from a peer. The mailing should detail what work the individual will do. In addition, it should identify how the money raised will be used and who will benefit.

The best procedure will bring the callers together for a period of time, include some training to establish objectives and procedures, and provide support to the callers as they work. Many times such a mini-phonathon can be run out of an office that has a sufficient number of phones close to each other.

Choosing a location

1. Separate offices prompt stress. Obviously, the first consideration is to have a location that has a sufficient number of phones to accommodate the workers. If the phones are in separate offices the callers will likely feel isolated, and each rejection will seem more personal since they will not see others in the same situation. As stress increases, the calls will come further apart and the workers will not likely return next year.

2. Two or three together promote conversations not calls. On the other hand, if two or three share a table the tendency will be for them to conclude calls at the same time and fall into conversation and loose efficiency. Such a situation also tends to be "too close for comfort" because there will be enough activity in the immediate area to mask individual conversations.

3. The ideal is a brokerage house "boiler room." In such an environment many people are in close proximity to each other, all doing the same thing. This creates a "team" of callers focused on one objective—completing as many successful calls as possible.

Creating atmosphere

1. Food. The most effective calling hours are between 7:00 and 9:00 in the evening. Calling before 7:00 risks interrupting dinner. After 9:00 could catch an early retiree in bed. Training will take about 20 minutes and should begin about 6:30. The most effective procedure is to ask the callers to come after work and provide a light supper of sandwiches and soup. Such a supper also contributes to the development of an *esprit de corps* and sets the evening off to a good start.

2. *"Entertainment"—post-success, use bells.* During the evening, keep spirits up by maintaining a running total of number of gifts received and total dollars pledged that evening. Also, have posted the previous evening's total, last year's totals, and this year's overall goal. Establish a goal for the evening based on the number of callers; in the second year base the goal on last year's total for that night.

Place a hotel desk call bell at each caller's phone. Have them ring the bell when they receive a pledge or need assistance. This will tend to keep the callers at their phones and working, and the ringing of the bells will create a force of their own. Reinforce the fact that their success is its own entertainment and reward.

3. *Rewards and recognition.* Many believe that their volunteers do not need special recognition. However, volunteers seldom refuse a $3 or $4 mug or school scarf when they secure the most pledges or raise the most dollars. It is the thought that counts; token rewards are in keeping with the spirit of the evening. To include more people give a prize for both the individual that gets the most firm pledges and for the individual who raises the most money. One affirms the bottom line and one affirms the need for broad based participation.

Recognizing workers through a picture in the press or through internal newsletters not only says thanks but also increases awareness of the program and the foundation's community roots.

Worker training

1. *Make it a positive and meaningful experience.* The first goal of worker training is to put the callers at ease with their

task. For the most part, they will be calling friends of the school district who support the foundation's goals. The callers do not have to be professional sales people to do a good job. Their task is to provide the prospect with the opportunity to be a part of a good thing.

The second goal is to place the evening's work within the context of the overall program. The workers are participating in a significant venture—the making of a better tomorrow through education.

2. *They are not there to browbeat their friends.* Training must dispel the popular notion that solicitation is an aggressive act that forces or manipulates the prospect into giving. It is no joking matter. The cause is important and each gift is essential to meeting common goals.

3. *Rehearse a call.* Time will not permit full blown role playing. Therefore, the trainer should recite a call from hello to goodby, carefully explaining the alternative responses to the prospect's decisions to give or not to give. Some people learn best from an oral presentation. Never assume new callers know how to solicit over the phone. Remember, most have never been in this situation before and need guidance.

4. *Have a script before them.* Provide a script callers might use for reference during their conversation. Some institutions put sample scripts on place mats that include possible responses to the most frequently asked questions and other pertinent data. Others prepare folders with such information inside.

5. *Listen to your callers as they begin and support those who show signs of stress.* Training is not completed until all workers are making calls and enjoying their experience. Move around the room and listen to the first calls. If you hear someone who sounds confused stay with that person until they feel comfortable. Most welcome suggestions and an opportunity to tell someone what happened. Callers also need assurance that they are doing a good job. Don't hover, but do make yourself available.

Managing the paperwork of the evening

1. *It takes two to handle an active phonathon.* One person should walk around answering the workers' questions and picking up the completed call forms. The second person should stay at a table and do the tabulation of the pledges, maintain a running tally of the evening's pledges for each worker, and total the number of gifts and dollars for the tally board. The tabulator should also place the pledge acknowledgements in the proper envelope for prompt mailing. Helpful equipment and materials would include pencils, an adding machine with tape read out, phone books, and, if alumni are called, phonathon yearbooks for the years being phoned. You will need a large blackboard upon which to post goals and updates as the evening progresses.

Preparing the prospect to receive the call

1. *Pre-phonathon mailing.* Each prospect to be called should receive within two weeks of the phonathon a letter explaining that the phonathon is coming and giving the specific dates volunteers will be calling. If available, it would also be helpful to identify those working the phonathon. In this letter the case for support should be presented in brief form and those who will benefit should be identified.

When calling on alumni, make an effort to secure the participation of alumni as callers. Ideally, a member of each class should sign the pre-phonathon letter being sent to his or her classmates. Always have a volunteer sign all pre-solicitation correspondence.

2. *Pre-phonathon promotion.* Because both the foundation and the phonathon are new, don't miss the opportunity to inform a broader constituency than the identified pros-

pects, using articles and pictures in the public media about the program and its leadership. This is the type of good news they will like.

Turning pledges into dollars

It would be nice to think that all those who pledge will honor their commitment without a reminder. However, reality forces a system of follow up. The following is a series of follow up procedures that should be considered.

1. Send pledge confirmation with return envelope the day following the phonathon.
2. Send first reminder in two months from phonathon.
3. Send second reminder six months from phonathon.
4. Send first letter reminder two months from close of fiscal year.
5. Call pledges over $50 one month from close of fiscal year.

Reaching the unreachable

No matter how effective the phonathon some prospects will remain after you finish. If the phonathon was well planned there should not be too many and not enough to schedule another round of phoning. Therefore, follow up with a mailing to those not reached that proceeds as follows:

Send a "sorry we missed you letter," including a response envelope within two weeks to all those who received the pre-phonathon mailing.

Send a "last chance to be included" letter one month from close of fiscal year.

Forms that think ahead:

1. Pledge and pledge reminder forms.
2. Bio information forms.
3. Worker performance forms.
4. Worker reminder postcard.

18 Organizing for special gift solicitation

Any effective special gift solicitation is always part of an overall program of constituency relations and fund raising. This has not always been the case. Historically, many charities were maintained through special gifts and the generosity of a few.

With the growth of a middle class that enjoyed the luxury of having discretionary income, the responsibility to fund organizations maintained in the public interest began to be shared by a wider group. Currently, despite the probability that 50 percent to 75 percent of money will be given by 10 percent of the donors, those few donors will disappear if their giving is not reinforced by the giving of a wide group.

What is a special gift program?

A special gift program focuses on a relatively small portion of the foundation's constituency. It asks, through a special cultivation and solicitation process, that individuals consider making large, one time gifts, usually to fund a specific program or facility.

What will a special gift program do?

A well-run special gift program will raise large gifts. It should not be asked to do anything more. Part of the program will require plans and procedures for distributing information to, and involving the prospects. However, these tasks must be undertaken with a specific prospect in mind rather than the needs of a group.

What will a special gift program not do?

It will not:

1. Broaden the base of donors.
2. Involve a large group of people.
3. Allow use of *any* good worker.
4. Dispel fears about elitism.

Identify prospects to be considered

1. Gather prospect's name and pertinent data.
2. Look for relationships, then dollars.

The first solicitation task is to identify the prospects. Relative affluence is one place to begin when developing a prospect list, but only one. A more telling factor will likely be the individual's personal relationship with the district. In fact, begin the search with a list of individuals who have been specially served by the district in the recent past. Ask people of affluence within that group to participate in a special gift program, both as worker and as donor.

Leadership essential to special gift solicitation

When considering possible structures for a special gift solicitation, plan so that the special gift program does not conflict with other programs and procedures, and is accorded the level of institutional support needed to make it effective. To be effective, staff, fund raising volunteers, board members (both school board and foundation board) must work together as a team. For that to happen affirm roles and carefully define job and reporting responsibilities.

The role of the school board

Unlike many other programs the foundation might undertake, the initiation of a special gift solicitation will require the understanding and support of the school board. Large gifts are made to causes only when the donors believe that they will be well used. How many donors ask for an accounting from an institution to which they give $25.00? However, as our commitment increases and the cause becomes a key charity among those we support, our concern for the detail increases.

Because a gift to the foundation is a gift to the school district, the attitude of the school board will be critical. The community leaders who will be essential to the success of the foundation will encounter other community leaders and members of the school board. Should they be told by a school board member at a cocktail party that the foundations programs are insignificant the potential for a large gift will be reduced.

Ideally, the school board would believe deeply in the mission of the foundation. Former school board members should provide a strong prospect pool for the foundation board.

The strongest solicitation team would contain a member of the foundation board who brings with him or her a member of the current school board. The foundation board member and the school board member could testify to the effectiveness of the foundation in supporting the programs of the district.

President of the foundation board

The role of the president of the foundation board changes little in response to a special gifts program—it only becomes more critical. The president of the board presides over the governing body that is responsible for the overall operating success of the foundation. Successful programs prompt large gifts.

The president leads the board in setting foundation policy and overseeing its implementation. The most critical job of the president is to ensure the quality of the process, that leads to the definition of the campaign goals. The process must be open and inclusive, concluding with a clear and realistic vision. In addition, the process must generate a strong sense of ownership of that vision on the part of the board and key leadership of the foundation, including staff. (See chapter 13)

An equally critical role for the president of the board and the foundation is to make the first or second gift to the campaign. No rules, written or unwritten, govern how much the board president must give. The only essentials are that the gift be made early in the campaign, that it represent a real effort on the part of the president to reach the goal, and that the foundation be numbered among the top of the leaders list of charities.

As stated, an effective special gift solicitation will be a part of a larger program. Therefore, it is likely that the chair of special gifts will report to a general campaign chair and function as part of an overall campaign committee.

Campaign leadership

The campaign committee receives goals from the school board and foundation board that: 1) have been unanimously certified to be essential to fulfilling the mission of the foundation; 2) are believed to represent attainable programs; 3) will be supported by a foundation board whose individuals are prepared to make an appropriate contribution to ensure success. Wise volunteer leadership will always refuse to accept appointments until all of the above is in place, for success depends on the depth of leadership's commitment to achieving the goal.

Role of the chair of the campaign

The first role of the chair is to decline the appointment until satisfied that the essential leadership is properly postured in relation to the goals of the program. Second, the chair must endorse the conclusions of the district's leadership. Finally, the chair must assume the responsibility of giving a leadership gift in an amount appropriate to the individual's level of commitment and relative affluence.

The administrative or executive role of the chair is to preside over the committees that develop the plans and procedures for running the campaign. Although the previous fund-raising experiences of the chair will be helpful, it is not the responsibility of the campaign chair to know enough about development programs to come up with the plan. The job of the chair is to know and understand the foundation's constituency well enough to identify the best program when presented with alternatives by staff.

The working role of the chair is: 1) to enlist the volunteers necessary for the task, and 2) to supervise the work of the volunteers to a successful conclusion.

Beyond the willingness to give an appropriate personal gift, the chair must possess a number of key qualities such as those listed below. To reach its goals the campaign will need people with all those characteristics. However, no one can be expected to possess them all.

When selecting a chair select:

credibility	over	cleverness
negotiator	over	influence
focus/time	over	power
sincerity	over	glibness

Role of the chair of special gifts

The job of the special gift committee, especially the chair, is to give and get dollars. If your campaign runs true to the norm, this committee will raise 75 percent to 90 percent of the dollars from no more than 10 to 20 percent of the donors.

The tasks associated with this chair are: 1) solicit and enlist the members of the major gift committee, 2) conduct committee meetings necessary to maintain contact with and support of the work of the volunteers, 3) see the effective training of the volunteers, and 4) provide extra support to those who find it difficult to accomplish the assigned tasks. The chair of special gifts should be able to speak sincerely of his or her commitment to the foundation.

Role of the constituency chairs

The constituency chairs will be the key spokesperson for the campaign from within their constituency. The chairs and their committees, made up of others from that constituency, will see to the general ambience within their peer group. As with all other special gift leaders, this individual must also make a substantial gift commensurate with ability to give.

The tasks associated with this position are:

1) solicitation and enlistment of individuals from among his or her constituency to accomplish the identification, cultivation, and solicitation of individual special gift prospects.

2) work with the solicitors in accomplishing their tasks providing support and challenge.

The constituency chairs must be resourceful, able negotiators, focused, hard working, and able to speak with ease on the issues surrounding the special gifts solicitation.

Role of the staff

In house executive operational tasks:

1. Provide essential program orientation to volunteers to ensure the effectiveness of their work.

2. Support volunteer enlistment and solicitation calls when called upon.

3. Facilitate an accurate and timely flow of information: volunteer to institution; volunteer to volunteer; institution to volunteer; and institution to community.

4. Coordinate the work of support staff.

5. Ensure the effective maintenance of appropriate work calendars.

In house executive nonoperational tasks:

1. Serve as resource to the planning and goal setting process of the volunteer leadership in the general areas of volunteer involvement and fund raising.

2. Develop, with volunteers and support staff, strategies for implementing objectives identified by the volunteer leadership.

3. Monitor the implementation of related programs; identify problem areas and develop alternative strategies to compensate for weaknesses as they emerge.

4. Participate with volunteer and staff in the development of solicitation strategies for special gift prospects.

5. Provide training to volunteers in the techniques of enlistment and solicitation.

In house support staff tasks:

1. See to the development, retention, and availability of pertinent data on special gift prospects.

2. Prepare information and materials as needed to support the cultivation, enlistment, and solicitation activities of the volunteers.

3. Ensure the effective management of all events and activities related to the program.

Setting the goal

1. Define the needs of the district.
2. Establish potential by rating prospects and soliciting leadership.
3. Confirm potential by soliciting workers.
4. Foundation board must set goal after giving themselves.

Goal setting is really a process of self-evaluation undertaken by the volunteer leadership prior to beginning solicitation. Setting a goal is essential to effective special gift solicitation, and must be concentrated within the leadership of the special gifts program for they will be responsible for raising most of the money.

One begins with establishing what is needed to accomplish the program goals of the district. Those needs are then stated in terms of a dollar goal. Translating that trial goal into a scale of gifts defines what must be given by the lead donors. The next step is to develop, based upon that scale of gifts, an individual asking that could be presented to the prospects at the time of solicitation.

Identifying what would be a responsible asking for each individual often prompts a change in the goal. If there is no one to be asked to consider the top gifts needed as projected by a scale of gifts (chapter 3), the goal must be reviewed.

The rating process will affect how people view the goal at their own giving level. Both will change depending how the process is handled and how the volunteers respond—who says what to whom in what sequence will determine the outcome.

It is essential that leadership carefully monitor and control who is in the process together. All donor levels must eventually be a part, for all must play a role to achieve maximum results. However, as in solicitation, it is extremely important that peers relate to each other. The individual capable of giving $1,000 simply cannot project with accuracy the potential of an individual with a $100,000 capability.

This critical balancing of the volunteers must extend into donor attitudes as well as giving potential. Individuals with lesser resolve (prospects) in relation to the goal or the project must interact with those already committed (leaders), with those who have the respect of the prospect, and with those who possess the ability to express how they feel about the cause. Then the circles must be allowed to expand outward.

Timing is an essential management tool and must be used effectively in the goal setting, self-evaluation process. Each step outlined above represents a unique and essential step in the development of ownership. See chapter 5. The stronger and broader the ownership, the higher the goal will be. To rush the process will truncate the growth of the goal. To not keep it going will allow it to die.

Thus the time must come when someone says to someone else, "It is hoped that you will consider giving $_____." That process must always begin within the leadership. Those who set the goal must commit before asking anyone else to give.

The solicitation of the leadership forms the second testing of the trial goal. If a significant portion of the goal has not been met by the leadership, it is likely that the goal is too high.

Remember, people can not effectively ask for more than they are giving themselves. Therefore, if the leadership consists of all smaller donors, no one will be able to ask for the large gifts essential to success.

The final testing of the trial goal comes with the enlistment and accompanying solicitation of those who will be needed to work on the program—the callers who will be doing the footwork. If the majority do not give in the aggregate commensurate with the asking assigned the goal must be reviewed. If they meet or exceed the asking, the goal should be secure.

Getting started

This section assumes that the foundation has within its leadership the type and quantity of volunteers necessary for success.

The next element that must be in place is the definition of the individual programs that could be made possible through larger individual one time gifts. Such programs could be the purchase of special equipment or the endowment of special supporting programs, such as an art gallery. Generally look for discrete funding opportunities ranging from $5,000 to $100,000.

Finally, you need a prospect who will take the lead and make such a gift. Once that has happened the goal is to ask that individual to ask his or her peers to join with him or her and make even more possible.

Enlisting leadership

Once past the hurdle of securing the first gift, enlisting others to work in the program should follow the same procedures used when enlisting workers for any other program. Pre-enlistment procedures should include:

  a. Define the role of this leadership position within the structures of the program.

  b. Identify the specific tasks to be done, including an estimate of the time they will take.

  c. Develop individual job descriptions.

At the time of the actual enlistment one should:

  a. Use the job descriptions. It is useless and harmful to the volunteer and the cause to tell someone, "it will not require much."

b. Be specific—what needs to be done when.

c. Present giving and working as a package. One never substitutes for the other—both are required for success.

Organizational alternatives

There is no right organizational pattern—the one that works is the right one. However, some organizational patterns have proven effective for others. The key to each is organizing by peer group.

Obviously, each of us is part of several peer groups—age, affluence, neighborhood, social or business affiliations. Volunteer leadership must define which grouping will place people in contact with each other in the most meaningful way. Meaningful in this situation could focus on common history, and concentrate on solicitation by class for alumni and by school building for parents. Demographics of the community could determine that organizing by vocation or neighborhood would be preferable.

In all instances, it is important to begin having volunteers reporting to volunteers, not the development office or staff. A volunteer can say things to another volunteer that staff would find difficult. Start with the pyramid concept of a chair who enlists captains who in turn enlist workers. Such a structure will accomplish more and develop the volunteer ownership essential for success.

Recognizing support

Why recognize supporters? It is in the institution's self-interest. Properly done, it provides the volunteer leadership with information concerning how his or her investment in the organization paid off in the lives of others. Also, employ donor clubs and conduct donor club activities.

19   Planned giving: Where the big money is

by Leonard G. Clough

Introduction

If you were to pay all your outstanding bills today, what would your check book balance be?

How would you respond to a request which came in today's mail for a contribution to strengthen public education in your community?

Many would reply: "Sorry. Much as I would like to help, I just can't afford it right now."

Those who are fortunate enough to have a healthy balance in their checking account after paying bills probably are worried about their financial security in the years ahead.

Result? Instead of sending a check for $1,000, they might send $10, $25, or even $100. The rest would probably go into a savings account or a money market fund.

When we analyze our own financial situations and those of others whom we know, it is easy to understand why public education and other good causes must find new ways to secure financial support from concerned individuals.

Planned giving is one of the most promising of these new methods.

What is planned giving?

Planned giving is a program enabling many people to bene-fit charities of their choices by making generous gifts from their accumulated assets. Usually these gifts are much larger than the donor would consider making as an out-right gift.

Miss Baker, an 82-year-old retired school teacher who lives on limited fixed income, is a good example.

When she receives request for annual gifts from some of her favorite charities, she usually sends checks ranging from $5 to $25.

Recently Miss Baker withdrew $5,000 from a savings ac-count that was paying her interest at the rate of 5½ percent per year.

She sent her $5,000 check to a pooled income fund, which is operated by a community foundation. For the rest of her life she will receive quarterly checks that will vary de-pending upon the income earned by that pooled income fund. It is currently paying 10 percent.

Miss Baker would like to have given $5,000 outright to support educational work in the community where she has invested most of her life as a school teacher. However, she felt that she needed the income that $5,000 would be pro-ducing in the years ahead. She was delighted to find that she had nearly doubled her income from that asset by transferring it from her savings account to a pooled income fund.

She was also pleased to learn that when she filed her fed-eral income tax return for that year, she would be able to claim a substantial charitable contribution deduction, which would make her income tax bill smaller, thus leaving her with more money to spend for other things.

Miss Baker had not been worrying about estate taxes, but she was pleased to learn that upon her death there would be less possibility of any estate taxes being due. Her gift of $5,000 had reduced her taxable estate by that amount.

At the time of Miss Baker's death, the community foundation will honor her request to have her gift made available for educational work in that community. The exact amount will depend upon the value of her units in the pooled income fund at the time of her death. The chances are excellent that they will be worth more than the $5,000 she had originally transferred.

The properly conceived and managed planned giving program will offer several types of planned gifts to meet the particular financial needs of various donors.

Some donors are primarily concerned about increasing their income from appreciated, low yield investments. Others want to avoid unnecessary income taxes, estate taxes, gift taxes or capital gains taxes. Still others have as their primary goal the ability to pass on valuable property to family or friends without having that gift seriously eroded by gift taxes or estate taxes.

Whichever type of life income gift a donor may select, he or she also has the satisfaction of having made a much larger gift than would otherwise have been possible.

What are some of the ways a planned giving program can help increase financial support?

Provide Endowment Funds

Many universities, hospitals, symphony orchestras, and other non-profit organizations have discovered that bequests and life income gifts are becoming the source of their largest gifts for endowment purposes.

Capital Campaigns

One of the most recent developments in fund raising is the increasing amount of money raised for major capital campaigns through planned giving.

The most obvious use would be in inclusion of endowment funds in a capital campaign to maintain buildings whose initial cost is paid from outright gifts to the campaign.

It is possible for an institution to use charitable remainder trusts and other planned giving contracts as collateral for loans to pay construction expenses.

Some capital campaigns fund long-term planning which will not require major amounts until some future date.

Memorial Funds

Some donors prefer to make bequests or life income gifts to memorialize a friend or a loved one.

Annual Giving

In most cases planned gifts do not become available to an institution until some time in the future. However, when gift annuities are reinsured, the gift portion becomes available to the institution immediately. If an insurance policy is contributed, the institution usually has the privilege of cashing it in at any time.

Some charitable organizations possessing planned giving programs have discovered that donors who first ask for information about a life income gift or bequest decide to make an immediate gift.

How can a public school or a public school system initiate a planned giving program?

If there is nobody on the staff or board who is familiar with planned giving techniques, it is sometimes possible to get helpful advice and counsel from the staff or board members of nearby institutions having a planned giving program. Professional planned giving consultants who work on a fee basis are increasingly available to provide assistance in the planning and development of a successful planned giving program.

1. The first step is to obtain all available information for use by the policy making board.

They are certain to ask questions such as these: What reason is there to believe a planned giving program will help us? How would planned gifts be secured and administered? How much would it cost?

2. The second step would be for the top policy making board to take official action to authorize, fund, and delegate responsibility for the administration of a planned giving program.

To qualify as a charity to which donors may make tax deductible gifts, a public school or public school system needs to consider using a local community foundation as a recipient of gifts or to consider establishing a special foundation that qualifies.

3. The next step would be to provide adequate staff, to retain legal counsel, and to secure whatever approvals are required in a given state by the IRS and other governmental bodies.

4. Recruiting a planned giving committee should be the next step. Ideally, this committee will consist of people who are not only deeply concerned about the financial future of a given public school or public school system, but also have professional expertise enabling them to give technical advice to staff and also to open doors from time to time to potential donors.

Lawyers who are involved in estate planning and estate settlements, accountants, trust officers, life insurance agents, financial planners and others who are directly or indirectly involved in financial planning procedure make excellent members of a planned giving committee.

5. Once the proper groundwork has been lain, it is time to begin marketing the planned giving program. This involves basic interpretive material, which may be in printed form and in audio-visual form.

Direct mail, which includes letters and carefully prepared printed materials, can evoke responses from people who would like to know more about ways a planned giving program might benefit them as well as the school or school system.

Public media, such as newspapers, radio, television, and especially cable television, should be used to inform people about the possibilities offered by a planned giving program.

In many communities, seminars that provide an introduction to personal financial planning are an excellent way to meet the needs of people and to discover who some of the potential donors might be. These seminars can include brief presentations by a lawyer who explains what happens when people die without a valid will, how to choose an executor or executrix, how much it costs to have a will drawn, how often a will should be reviewed. Following a lawyer's presentation, a question period will permit those present to determine most of the agenda.

A trust officer might be asked to make a brief presentation explaining the various ways trusts can help people meet their needs and why one does not have to be a millionaire to use a trust.

A representative of your school or school system would then explain how your planned giving program fits into personal financial planning for people who are concerned about the future financial health of your school or school system.

An insurance representative or an investment advisor might be the fourth speaker.

Experience has shown that including a representative from the Social Security Administration will also be deeply appreciated and provide information that most people have never bothered to acquire.

These and other methods of finding potential donors should prompt personal visits by representatives of the school or school system to persuade donors to make a gift, and if so, which type of gift would be best for them.

6. At the end of each year the planned giving program should be evaluated and necessary changes should be made in marketing methods.

What does a potential planned giving donor look like?

A potential donor tends to be the one who has the following characteristics:

1. Has expressed interest in your school or educational program over a period of several years.

2. Has few financial dependents.

3. Is more than 50 years old.

4. Has accumulated financial assets. These may be in the form of bank accounts, money market funds, real estate, stocks and bonds, boats, stamp collections.

A SUMMARY OF THE MOST COMMON PLANNED GIVING INSTRUMENTS

Type of Gift	Form of Gift	Size of Gift	Advantages to Donor (in addition to satisfaction of making a gift and reduction of taxable estate)	Advantages to Your Org.
I. Outright Gifts	–Cash –Securities –Real Estate –Insurance Policies	Unlimited	–100% deductible for income tax	–Funds are available for immediate use by your organization
II. Charitable Lead Trusts	–Cash –Securities –Real Estate	Usually $100,000 or more.	–Allows property to be passed to others with little or no shrinkage due to taxes	–Provides current income for period of at least ten years
III. Life Income Gifts (Irrevocable)				
A. Gift Annuities	–Cash –Securities	$1,000 to $5,000 minimum	–Guaranteed, fixed income –Excellent tax deduction when reinsured –Some tax-free annual income	–When reinsured, provides "now" money for your organization –Minimal administrative work and costs
B. Deferred Payment Gift Annuities	–Cash –Securities	$1,000 to $5,000 minimum	–Tax deduction during high income years –Guaranteed retirement income later	–Same as Gift Annuity
C. Pooled Income Fund Agreements	–Appreciated Securities –Cash	$1,000 to $5,000 minimum	–Variable income that may provide hedge for inflation –No capital gains tax liability on gift –Tax deduction when gift is made	–Assures future funding for work of your organization
D. Charitable Remainder Unitrusts	–Real Estate –Securities –Cash	Usually $50,000 minimum	–Same as Pooled Income Fund plus: –Can be tailored to donor's situation –Permits deferred income if desired –Excellent for gifts of real estate	–Assures substantial future funding for work or your organization –Donor of your organization may select Trustee –Your organization may be able to use trust as collateral for loans
E. Charitable Remainder Annuity Trusts	–Cash –Securities	Usually $50,000 minimum	–Fixed income –Tax deduction in year gift is made –No capital gains tax on appreciated gift –May provide tax-free income	–Same as Unitrusts

Type of Gift	Form of Gift	Size of Gift	Advantages to Donor	Advantages to Your Org.
IV. Revocable Charitable Trusts	-Cash -Securities -Real Estate	Usually $50,000 minimum	-All or part of amount placed in trust is available if needed by donor -Removes work and worry of managing assets	-Very high percentage of revocable trusts are not revoked, thus giving promise of future funding for work of your organization
V. Insurance Policies				
A. When your organization is made owner and beneficiary of continuing policy	- - -	Unlimited	-Donor gets income tax deduction for value of policy when transferred -Premium payments may be deducted as gift -Donor can make large gift in future at small cost now	-Upon death of insured, your organization will receive face value of policy. Your organization may borrow on policy. Your organization may cash in policy
B. Giving paid-up policies		Unlimited	-Tax deduction based on current value of policy	-You may keep policy and receive face value upon death of insured -You may borrow on policy -You may cash in policy
C. Name your organization as beneficiary but not as owner		Unlimited	-Enables donor to make large future gift at small cost -Donor may change beneficiary later -Donor may borrow on policy	-Upon death of insured, you will receive face value of policy

(Special Note: Life insurance may also be used to replenish the donor's estate for amounts given for a life income gift. Donor receives life income. Gives enough to someone else each year to pay premiums of life insurance policy on the donor. Upon death of donor, your organization receives life income gift; family or others receive insurance proceeds. Double mileage!)

VI. Bequests

Anything one owns at the time of death may be passed on to your organization or to anyone else through one's last will and testament.

All forms of life income gifts listed above (Section III) may be made in testamentary form to benefit family or friends and then will become available for use by your organization.

20 Sponsored programs

by Ruth McClellan Killoran

Sponsored programs suffer from a definite identity problem. Persons unfamiliar with our profession often ask me
what I do—or more often—what's a sponsored program?
My usual answer to this query is, "I deal with grants." To be
a little more specific, sponsored programs are those projects your institution has chosen to fund externally. The
funding can come from a variety of sources—government
(federal, state), foundations, corporations, other organizations or individuals. The programs can run the gamut from
scholarship aid and training programs to building campaigns and equipment requests. In the case of elementary
and secondary schools, a program could include funding a
special trip for a class, a scholarly publication for a teacher
or administrator, part of the operating budget, equipment,
a new approach to teaching a particular subject or subjects
or almost any area that relates to school operation. Some
ideas are naturally more fundable than others!

So what exactly is fundable and how do you find that
out? What do you do first—write a proposal or look for a
funding source? How do you develop an idea for a grant?
The next few pages will deal with the proposal idea, the
groups who actually fund these ideas, where you can get
the information you need, the necessary research process,

the technicalities of proposal writing, and grants administration in general. The purpose of this section is to demystify the grants process and show you how to find external dollars for your school.

The proposal idea

Let's assume you have been asked to find some grant money to help fund a new reading program. Now you can go ahead and find a sponsor. Can you? Why does the school want or need a new reading program? What will it do exactly? What's being done now? Who will do it, what are their qualifications, and how much will this cost?

It is important at this initial stage to sit down with the requesting party or a group who will be involved in the project and do some preliminary planning. To proceed in the grants process, you need much more information than that given originally. Although you will not be writing the proposal for some time, you need to develop a concept paper or prospectus of your intentions. This will assist you greatly as you trudge through the grants process.

Basically, the concept paper should include the following: a statement of the problem, how you intend to solve the problem, the objectives of the project, your qualifications to carry out the project, and how much it will cost. This does not have to be long—it can be as short as one page or can run several pages.

The importance of this summary paper cannot be overstated. It accomplishes several things: 1) forces the person or group to really think through the idea; 2) underscores the credibility of your organization; 3) gives an estimate of the cost; and 4) can be used to consider whether the program is within the priorities of the organization. You will need this information as you consider the various funding options and as you proceed in the marketing of your idea. Additionally, the concept paper process helps to assure that the proposed project is something in which the group really wants to get involved.

So who will fund such an idea?

So you've developed your idea and have put together a concept paper. Now what? Who are those mysterious people who give out grant money? Basically they are the federal government, state governments, foundations, corporations, and individuals. Although individuals do give money for various projects, they are not usually part of the sponsored programs effort. The discussion, therefore, will concentrate on the other four categories.

The Federal government

The U.S. government is still the biggest single source of financial aid even though there are no firm figures on the amount (since the figures are tabulated in so many different ways). The generally accepted figure is at least $100 billion annually. The federal government disburses its grant and contract dollars in a number of ways:

Project grants are funds set aside for very specific short-term projects or the delivery of specialized services, e.g. fellowships, scholarships, traineeships, publications, and research grants. These grants tend to be for one year.

Formula grants are funds for educational, health, and welfare services returned to local communities under general reserve sharing or directly allotted to states according to specific distribution formulas. These formulas are based on such demographics as the number of people in the state and how much they earn.

A *contract* is defined by the federal government as an instrument to procure research or some other type of work. A grant is defined as a mechanism to support such activity. Under contract, for example, are computer programs, training programs, and feasibility studies. Contracts require considerable time and organizational backup and are probably not as attractive to school systems as grants—where there is more flexibility.

A *block* (or bloc) grant is usually made to states or local communities for broad purposes as authorized by legislation. There is considerable flexibility in the distribution as long as the basic purposes are fulfilled.

Demonstration grants establish or demonstrate the feasibility of a theory or an approach.

Training grants are awarded to support the costs of training students, personnel, or prospective employees in research or in techniques or practices pertinent to a particular area of concern.

State government

State government departments disburse grant dollars through block grants, through other federal dollars passed to the state for administration, and through their own funds. States award both contracts and grants of all types.

Foundations

The Foundation Center defines a foundation as a "non-governmental, non-profit organization with funds and programs managed by its own trustees or directors and established to maintain or aid social, educational, charitable, religious, or other activities serving the common welfare, primarily through the making of grants." There are various types, namely:

Independent. Funds or endowments designated by the IRS as private foundations whose primary function is the making of grants. They are often called *family* foundations because most come from the gifts of one person or family and many function under the direction of family members.

Company. Independent grant making organizations even though they maintain close ties to the corporation providing the funds by means of endowment or by award contributions. Officers of the company as well as other persons may serve on their boards. Company sponsored foundations make grants on a broad basis as compared with corporate giving programs which tend to be more closely allied to the parent corporation.

Operating. Are private even though their primary purpose is to operate their own research, social welfare, or other program. Occasionally they may fund other agencies.

Community. Designated by the IRS as public, nevertheless, operate like private foundations. Their funds come from many donors rather than one source and funds are directed to their own localities.

The United States has approximately 22,000 foundations. In 1986 these foundations gave a record $5.17 billion to agencies, institutions, and organizations.

Corporations

Corporations gave over $4.5 billion to philanthropy in 1986, up from half a billion twenty years ago. In 1979, business giving exceeded foundations' giving for the first time.

Today corporations give because they feel social responsibility, because it is a good form of advertising, and because it improves their image. Their giving may be restricted to the areas where they operate and it is usually part of their corporate planning strategy.

How do you find out about these funding sources?

The library has the most information on all these funding sources. Most main and/or state libraries will have books pertaining to corporations, the federal government and to a certain extent, foundations. University libraries may also have the reference material you need. The best place for foundation research is the Foundation Center, 79 Fifth Avenue, New York, New York 10003 or one of its satellite offices:

The Foundation Center
Kent H. Smith Library

739 National City Bank Bldg.
1422 Euclid
1444 Hand Building
Cleveland, Ohio 44114
216/861-1933

The Foundation Center
312 Sutter Street
San Francisco, CA 94108
415/397-0902

The Foundation Center
1001 Connecticut Avenue, N.W.
Washington, D.C. 20036
202/331-1400

For cooperating collections in other states, call the Foundation Center toll free at 800/424-9836.

Information can also be gathered from the persons in the business, from those who have received grants, and from the funding sources themselves. It is imperative to make contacts and sustain them, for people are one of your most important sources.

The Research tools for foundations

The Foundation Center has done a splendid job of assembling materials on foundations and has made foundations comparatively easy to research. The books which you will need, follow. If you plan to continue to seek funding, it would be to your advantage to have them as part of your basic library.

1. The *Foundations Grants Index,* New York: The Foundation Center. Included are grants of $5,000 and over awarded by major foundations in the United States.

2. *Comsearch Printouts,* New York: The Foundation Center. These publications include grants of $5,000 or more made to nonprofit organizations and reported to the Foundation Center by over 400 foundations. Comsearch Printouts have detailed indexing and provide overviews of major foundations in your area of interest.

3. The *Foundation Directory*, New York: The Foundation Center. This book includes descriptive entries for all foundations with assets of $1 million or grants totaling $100,000 or more annually.

4. *Source Book Profiles*, New York: The Foundation Center. These give detailed profiles of the 1,000 largest foundations.

5. *The Annual Report*. Many, but not all foundations, publish an annual report. The annual report is the best, most accurate source of information on a foundation. You can get it by writing or calling the foundation.

6. *990 Forms*—every foundation must file a 990 with the IRS. These reports indicate what their assets are, how much they gave away and to whom. Trustees of the foundation are also included.

7. *National Data Book*, New York: The Foundation Center. This lists almost all the 25,000 foundations in the United States. It is useful to identify small foundations in your locale.

8. *Trustees of Wealth*, Washington, D.C.: J. Richard Taft Co. Included are biographies on foundation officers and trustees. This can be useful when planning a visit to a foundation.

9. *Magazines and newspapers—Foundation News, Grantsmanship Center News, New York Times, Wall Street Journal, Forbes, Business Week, Time, Newsweek, U.S. News and World Report*. Some of these are directed at foundations while others may only occasionally mention them. They do, however, provide a good overview for understanding both foundation and corporate philanthropy.

10. *Taft Foundation Information System*, Washington, D.C.: The Taft Corporation. This includes the *Taft Foundation Reporter*, and two monthly publications, *Foundation Giving*

Watch and *Foundation Updates*. The *Reporter* has profiles on the most important foundations while the two monthlies interpret news of the foundation world in a timely fashion.

Research tools for corporations

Information on corporations is not as easily available. There are some subject directories but they may not necessarily be up-to-date. The Better Business Bureau has files on many corporations and their grant giving activity. The local chamber of commerce should have lists of corporate contributors in your area. The office of the attorney general or the county clerk's office in your state may have records on corporate foundations (since they are tax exempt). The offices of trade associations and other groups have industry studies, membership rosters, and analyses of national trends in funding. The following books can be useful:

Corporate Directory, Washington, D.C.: Taft Corporation. Reports on 441 corporate foundations. It has indexes by state, fields of interest, corporate operating locations, names, sponsoring companies, and types of grants.

Directory of Corporate Affiliations, Skokie, Illinois: National Register Publishing House. Tells you who owns what and helps identify corporate subsidiaries.

Standard and Poor's Register of Corporations, Directors and Executives, New York: Standard and Poor's Corporation, annual. Provides corporate addresses, telephone numbers, names and brief biographies of executives.

Million Dollar Directory, New York: Dun and Bradstreet Corporation, annual, 3 volumes (covers corporations with sales over $1 million). Gives name, geographic area, and product classification.

Moody's Manuals—Provide extensive information on the history of corporations, financial data, and lengthy lists of corporate officers.

Research tools for government

A lot has been printed about federal government programs. You may have to consult more than one source to get all you want. In addition, in the case of the *Federal Catalog of Domestic Assistance*, it is out-of-date when printed, so you must double check all data.

> *Federal Catalog of Domestic Assistance*, Washington, D.C.: Executive Office of the President, Office of Management and Budget, annual. This is the most comprehensive of all books on federal government funding and lists all programs for state and local governments, territories of the United States, counties, cities, municipalities, public and private institutions, profit and non profit organizations, special interest groups and individuals. Though large, it is well indexed and a must for the grant seeker. It does not, however, include federal revenue sharing programs, automatic payment programs, foreign aid, solicited contracts or certain programs.

> *U.S. Government Manual*, Washington, D.C.: U.S. Government Printing Office, annual. This is a guidebook to the federal government and its agencies. It includes names of senior officials and organizational charts.

> *The Federal Register*, Washington, D.C.: U.S. Printing Office, daily. The most up-to-date source on agency rules and regulations including grant announcements. These announcements can also be found in various newsletters which may be easier reading.

> *Federal Contracts and Grants Weekly*, Arlington, VA: Capital Publications, Inc., weekly. This weekly publication summarizes much of what is in *The*

Federal Register. You may want to refer to the *Register,* however, for more information.

Mailing Lists—Many federal agencies such as the National Science Foundation and National Endowment for the Humanities have newsletters, grants announcements, etc. Write and ask to be on their lists.

State

Information about state funding is very difficult to find. Some states publish a guide similar to the *Federal Catalog of Domestic Assistance.* This will be at your state library.

The State Budget—This can be an overwhelming document, but it does provide information about state funding priorities. Also located at your state library.

The research process

Now you know where all this information is, so what do you do with it? The research of funding sources is fundamental to your grant seeking effort. Without it, you will miss many opportunities. It is time consuming, but rewarding and it can even be fun.

Foundations

The Foundation Center has helped to make foundation research a joy. In the previous section, I discussed the various publications which come into play. The research process is as follows:

1. Develop a broad list of prospects—use the *Comsearch Printouts* or *Foundation Grants Index* keeping in mind which foundations have indicated an interest in your subject area. The Fields of Interest Index in the *Foundation Directory*

and the Subject Index in *Source Book Profiles* can also be useful.

2. Narrow list by eliminating foundations whose own restrictions rule out funding your project. For example, do they give in your geographic area?

3. Research further—Consider subject interest, geographic preference, range of giving, type of support, type of recipient, application deadlines. Use *Source Book Profiles,* foundation annual reports, and 990 AR and 990 PF forms. Remember you are looking for a potential match between a foundation and your school. You are trying to determine if this foundation wants to give to your type of organization and your type of project. Is there a match? Your previously developed concept paper will come in handy here.

When you have narrowed your list, study it again. You will have additional questions. Now is the time to pick up the telephone and call the contact person for that foundation. If you feel there is a mutual interest, you will want to request an appointment. You may or may not be successful in this endeavor but, in any event, you can get lots of information over the phone by simply engaging the person in dialogue.

Foundations are being swamped with requests for visits these days. If you feel there is a good match between you and the foundation, you should try hard to arrange a meeting between their representative and one or two of your officials (perhaps the superintendent of schools and a PTA volunteer or a member of the board of education and a member of the PTA). There is no substitute for talking directly with foundation representatives.

Both your PTA and your board of education member should be invited to help with the grants process. They may know foundation trustees, or they may know about certain foundations. Your entire volunteer network should be tapped for pertinent information.

Corporations

The corporate research process is much less scientific than that for foundations. You will be able to get facts on giving priorities for some companies from the various directories mentioned previously. In addition, these will mention a corporate contributions person. You will want to call him or her to check the information you have, as well as to answer other questions such as: Is the company interested in giving to public schools? Are they interested in certain projects? What is the procedure for application? If the company has a local branch, you will want to call the manager of that organization to determine what your best approach is or, better yet, if they have a separate fund for philanthropy. Your volunteers who may know corporation officials can be very helpful in opening the right doors for you.

As with foundation officials, you should arrange an appointment to talk directly with the manager or the corporate contributions person. Again, several members of your organization—perhaps a staff member and a volunteer (preferably one who knows the company) should plan to go. Your concept paper will be very useful, particularly as a sales tool. In fact, your concept paper becomes your case.

You will want to draw upon your contacts in developing a dossier on corporations—probably more so than with any other constituency. Your aim is to tap into their networks through your volunteers or through anyone interested in your cause.

Federal government

There is an abundance of material available on federal grant dollars. Your objective is to sort what you need from the information you don't need.

If you are starting from scratch, i.e. your school is not yet on government agency mailing lists, the place to start is the *Federal Catalog of Domestic Assistance*. First, read the section "How to Use the Catalog" then turn to the Applicant Eligibility Index, look for the program numbers here and in the Subject Index as well. You can then turn to the description section of the catalog to determine your eligibility, restrictions, or anything that may exclude you or your idea.

Your next step is to contact the information person listed. Ask for current guidelines, eligibility requirements, amount of money available for the program, and application forms. Discuss your ideas with the funding official. Gauge his/her reaction to it. Is the agency interested in funding such projects? Will they review a draft of your proposal?

After receiving the guidelines and applications from the agency, you will have further questions. Call the agency again before you decide whether to proceed.

Federal program officers are usually happy to discuss your idea personally. If your budget permits, a trip to Washington is most desirable. This official can suggest other government departments who may be interested in your concept if it appears you do not have a match with this agency.

Other sources of information include groups who have been funded (ask the program officer for a list). You can also request copies of funded proposals. Some agencies will mail them while others have them available in their offices.

State government

Since there is so little available in writing about state funding, you will need to immediately go to your information contacts. Do they know of available funds? Who are the contact people? If the information is not available through this route, get a state government telephone directory and start calling departments. This is *very* time consuming. The alternate method is preferred.

Writing the proposal

Foundation and federal proposals will differ greatly in their final format, but the elements are the same. Usually, foundation proposals are short (e.g. a three to four-page letter with several appendices), while a federal proposal with required forms and attachments may run between 50 and 100 pages. The following is a basic outline of a proposal.

Introduction

Your introduction will include information about who you are, how your organization got started, anything that is unique about you, significant accomplishments and, in general, any information which gives your group credibility. Building credibility is vital to the development of your proposal. The introduction can also indicate your awareness of the interests of the foundation and how this proposal addresses these areas.

Problem or needs statement

Having used the introduction to set the context for your problem, this section can be used to describe the problem as well as your solution—including program objectives.

If you have defined the problem, then the objectives will address the solution. The objectives should be clear, measurable outcomes of your program. Good objectives serve another purpose in that you have established a set of criteria which can be used for evaluation purposes.

Methodology

This section deals with your solution to the problem—how you are going to attain the desired results and what activities will accomplish your objectives. Of course, you will want to demonstrate that you are knowledgeable about the field and that you know who else is doing work in this area. You will want to include the methods that have been tried and the results.

It is also important to show you have considered several ways to attack the problem, and give the reasons you chose the one you did.

Evaluation

Evaluation is essential for program proposals and should be addressed in a separate section. The objectives which you outlined previously can be used as the basis for an effective evaluation. If you have trouble determining what criteria to use to measure your program, better take another look at your objectives. They may need to be more specific.

Future funding

You will want to include a section on the continuation of your project. How will it be funded when the grant money is gone?

Follow up—whether you get the proposal or not

Previously we discussed the grants process. Let's assume you have developed a proposal idea, researched it to the best of your ability, submitted a proposal, and have been funded. First of all—congratulations! Secondly, don't think that all work and worries are over. You must of course implement your proposal. And you must report to the funding source.

Federal funding agencies will be very specific about the type and timing of reports. You may have interim and final accountings—both performance and financial. It is important to submit these in a timely fashion for you are building your reputation with an eye to future funding. Your next grant may very well come from a former donor.

Foundations may not be as specific as to the type of information they would like you to send. However you may be sure that they want it. When you receive notice of your award, call or write your contact person and ascertain what is required.

If you are turned down, don't think this is the end. Find out why you were not funded. Perhaps, with some modifications, you can resubmit the same proposal next year. At any rate, you now know more about that agency, foundation, or corporation than you did when you started. Your cultivation of that group has begun.

Cultivation is important for all constituencies, but particularly so for foundations. They often want to get to know you before they will fund your school. Thus you will want to contact them again, particularly if you plan to resubmit.

In either case, whether you are funded or not, you are now a knowledgeable person in the world of grants. The ground work has been established. Your concept is firm, the research has been done and the proposal written. At this point, you may want to go back to your research for other funding sources or, as indicated previously, wait to submit to the same agency next year. Or it may be time to start work on yet another idea!

Systems for sponsored programs

The work of research and follow up for sponsored programs generates tons of paper! I employ a variety of systems and charts to control the paper flow. Much, if not all of this, could be computerized if desired.

I monitor a number of topics in this process. For example, our research of foundations produces much information. At the same time, faculty and staff have requested possible sources for their proposal ideas. We organize this information in a 4 × 8 file box divided into two sections. The first is for foundation information which is recorded on a main card (see exhibit 1) and the second section is cross referenced by topic and faculty member. We place the actual research materials in the appropriate foundation file, but we can easily identify exactly what research has been completed and what is in process.

I use a regular tickler file. This file is broken down by day of the month (for the current month) and all the other months of the year. It helps to keep track of federal funding dates, and almost anything that will be occurring over the next year or two. The tickler is checked on a daily basis. Material placed in the tickler is returned to me when it is needed. I find that a perpetual calendar is a great asset as well. I use it mainly for upcoming proposal deadlines. The surface is shiny and information can be changed with a water based felt marker.

Other quick reference charts include one for targeted foundations and one for a cultivation plan. The targeted foundations are broken down by area of interest (see exhibit 2). The cultivation plan chart helps to keep track of what appointments need to be made and when. Actually the information on these charts can be found elsewhere but I keep these on a nearby bulletin board for easy reference as I do other planning.

We monitor all proposals sent out with a proposal log. The topic, amount, due date, cost sharing, and total amounts are shown here. This serves as a record of all proposals submitted (see exhibit 3).

Exhibit 1

Name: _____

Cross Referenced: _____

Purpose: _____

_____

_____

☐ research completed _____

☐ annual report _____

☐ telephone interview _____

☐ not viable at this time _____

☐ Development visit _____

☐ President visits _____

☐ call report _____

☐ proposal _____

accepts _____

rejects _____

Status: _____

Exhibit 2

Targeted Foundations

The following foundations are potential contributors and have been and are being cultivated.

Foundation	Capital Campaign	Computers	Faculty Development	Scholar-ships	Business Mngt.	Nursing Program	Health Program	Science Program	Alumni Giving

Exhibit 3

Prop. # Proj. Dir. Date Sub.	Title and Contract Period	Agency/ Foundation	Total Project Cost	Grant Request	Amount Received	Indirect Costs Realized	Contrib. Required	Cash Cost/ Not Budgeted	Antici. Notifi. Date	Disposition Award Date

21 Organizing a limited campaign

This chapter provides an outline covering the key elements of a short range fund raising campaign. This will be helpful for the institution wanting to raise money for a specific purpose with a one time campaign.

I.   *Goals of a fund raising program:*

A.   To develop a stronger school-family volunteer structure.

B.   To develop subgroup identity within the wider constituency, such as within classes or geographical regions.

C.   To strengthen individual ownership among the school family of the goals and mission of the district.

D.   To strengthen the pattern of individual outright giving to the broadest possible mission of the district rather than one time, special interest, or event centered fund raising projects.

If this is a first attempt at donor centered fund raising, this goal may have to be temporarily or partially set aside. First time donors are often more comfortable with designated giving. Initial leadership may not want to establish a full time development program, preferring at this time to conduct a one time trial campaign.

E.   To increase the percentage of donor participation.

II.   *Timing factors that influence a solicitation:*

A.   Parent campaigns are generally more successful if solicitation is conducted early in the fall, prior to the first report card and college acceptances.

B.   A lead gift campaign or personal solicitation in excess of $150 should be timed to allow the donor the advantage of two tax years in which to make the gift.

C.   The development of the volunteer fund raising structure must receive first priority, for it is more important than maintaining a schedule. Its development will ultimately determine the success of the campaign.

III. *Precampaign design process:*

A.   Goals of the planning and design phase of the campaign:
   1. Identify and enlist the best volunteers and the best leadership.
   2. Allow leadership to define its own goals in response to the needs of the institution.
   3. Develop a plan that enables the effective solicitation of as many individuals as possible.
   4. Set specific goals.

B.   Critique the past:
   1. Which individuals have expressed concern over what specific issues?
   2. Divide constituency into natural subgroups and identify solicitation leadership within each group.
   3. What was the response to each past organized volunteer activity and who responded?
   4. Which individual volunteers proved effective at what?

C.   Identify current potential:
   1. Rank identified constituency subgroups according to the number of volunteer workers with demonstrated ability to lead others.

2. Rank constituency subgroups according to giving potential: above average, average, below average. (Relative affluence or ability to give is subjective; therefore, analyze the individual evaluations for collective patterns).

3. Rank constituency subgroups according to their demonstrated readiness to be involved.

4. Merge the findings of B, C, and D and rank the subgroups from highest potential to least.

D. Involve a mix of volunteers from each subgroup and staff in the planning process. This is especially important when selecting which "target groups" will be solicited and in what way.

E. Planning must be an ongoing process. Volunteer workers must set their own goals and design their own procedures with counseling and support from more experienced volunteers and professionals.

IV. *Building volunteer ownership:*

A. Process is critical. Do not make significant decisions without involving the volunteers. People work better when they have developed the plan.

B. Volunteers must set overall and constituency goals only after they understand the needs and have first given themselves. Goals must be set in direct relationship to the giving patterns established by those setting the goal.

C. Volunteers must first solicit and then enlist their peers. Volunteers can not successfully solicit for gifts larger than they are giving. A prospect's gift size must be determined before an enlistment attempt.

D. Staff must not do a volunteer's predetermined task. If volunteers fall down, other volunteers must pick up the slack.

E. Volunteers must be held accountable by other committed and active volunteers, not by staff.

V.   *Campaign program components:*

A.   Prospect identification.

B.   Trial goal setting.

C.   Enlisting leadership
   1. Select leadership—never ask for volunteers
   2. Solicit leadership prospects before enlisting them. If they are not giving at a level that will challenge those whom they solicit, the program is probably critically, if not fatally, flawed.

D.   Thoroughly orient all volunteers regarding
   1. Needs to be met.
   2. Procedures to be employed.
   3. Role they are being asked to play.
   4. The time frame within which they are expected to perform their tasks.

E.   Final goal setting.

F.   Prospect Cultivation—Informing
   Communicating with prospects through mail, public and personal presentations regarding strengths and needs.

G.   Prospect Cultivation—Involving
   Involving individuals in any aspect of the school's programs.

H.   Define prospect solicitation methods to be used. (The following summary list is arranged in ascending order according to effectiveness.)
   1. General mailing which includes a response mechanism.
   2. Individual mailing with response mechanism.
   3. Phonathon, random calling.
   4. Phonathon, assigned calling.
   5. In person, group, followed by individual mail.
   6. In person, group, followed by individual phone.
   7. In person, group, followed by in person solicitation.
   8. In person, individual, peer-to-peer solicitation concluding with pledge.

I. Acknowledging and recognizing giving
    1. Say, "Thank you."
    2. Inspiring others and preparing this year's donors for next year's solicitation.

VI. *Campaign staff*

Many tasks must be accomplished if a fund raising program is to be successful. Generally those tasks are distributed between staff and volunteers according to whom is best equipped to do what. The activities most critical to success are enlistment and solicitation—both tasks must be assigned to the best volunteers. All other actions support those two central tasks.

In a start up situation there may not be any paid staff to support the campaign. Therefore, "staff" assignments listed below must also be distributed among a few specially selected volunteers.

In a campaign, the staff provides the following: (1) research, (2) clerical support, (3) communication, (4) volunteer coordination and monitoring, and (5) an orderly transition to next year's volunteer leadership.

VII. *Campaign sequence*

Staff/Volunteer Task 1—scheduled ASAP

Objective:
Develop the data essential to a thorough review of this year's potential (see section III).

Meeting 1—scheduled _____
                              (date)

Goal: Identify constituency subgroups and potential leadership within each.

Attendees: Development staff, appropriate school principals, chair of the campaign, outgoing chair if second campaign, development committee, president of the foundation.

Objectives:
1. Review potential using data collected on constituencies.

2. Select target groups within the District's constituencies.
3. Assign trial goals to each target group.
4. Identify and develop solicitation and enlistment strategies for leadership from within each target group to form annual fund committee.
5. Set goal for leadership's contribution to the campaign.
6. Assign individuals to solicit and enlist leadership.
7. Solicitors make their own commitments.

Staff Tasks 2 & 3—scheduled ASAP following meeting 1

Objectives Task 2:
1. Develop volunteer job descriptions for leadership positions identified in meeting 1.

Objectives Task 3:
1. Develop program alternatives and cost estimates for each target group to stimulate the planning process.
2. Send above to appropriate volunteer leader as soon as enlisted.

Volunteer Task 1—scheduled _____
                              (date)

Involving: Those in attendance at Meeting 1.

Objectives:
1. Solicit campaign leadership prospects.
2. Solicit and enlist campaign "target group" leadership.

Meeting 2—scheduled ASAP after Volunteer Task 1 is completed.

Goals: Orient leadership and initiate planning for target group programs.

Attendees: All of above plus president of school board, and target group leaders.

Objectives:
1. Chairman of the board places the campaign goals within the overall budget of the school.

2. Campaign chair introduces the leadership for this year's campaign and defines the general scope of their target group.
3. Break into one-on-one brainstorming session involving target group leader and staff/staff-trained volunteer.
4. Reconvene and continue brainstorming as a committee.
5. Conduct worker prospect rating.
6. Review target group goals.

NOTE. From this point on many of the tasks and meetings will be duplicated and/or modified to conform to the specific needs of the program being run among a specific target group.

Staff Task 4—schedule individual planning session with each target group leader ASAP after meeting 2.

Objectives:
1. Review data gathered through brainstorming.
2. Develop general plan to accomplish target group goal.
   a. Define cultivation activities.
   b. Define type of solicitation to be employed.
   c. Develop target group solicitation "theme".
3. Identify worker prospects.
4. Develop trial calendar.
5. Develop solicitation and enlistment strategies for worker prospects.

Volunteer Task 2—scheduled following staff task 4

Objectives:
1. Complete solicitation and enlistment strategies.
2. Report success to the development office.
3. Set time for worker orientation.

Staff Task 5—scheduled ASAP after staff task 4

Objective:
1. Prepare materials for target group program.

Meeting 3—scheduled after staff task 4 is completed.

Goals: Final committee planning session; approve working calendar; approve goals; approve working budgets.

Attendees: All listed in meeting 2.

Meeting 4—scheduled to allow for the enlistment of workers.

Goals: Conduct orientation/training session for workers.

Attendees: all above plus target group workers.

Objectives:
1. Orient workers to the need.
2. Orient workers to the procedures associated with the type of solicitation planned for their target group.
3. Distribute prospect cards.

Volunteer Task 3—scheduled ASAP following meeting 3.

Objectives:
1. Solicit assigned prospects.
2. Report results and problems back to development office.

Staff Task 5—scheduled during solicitation

Objective:
Contact workers to provide support and spot problems.

To help you in staffing positions for either a short or long run campaign, here are job descriptions for five key staff positions.

Job Description
Parent Special Campaign for Class Room Renovation

GENERAL CHAIR

ROLE

Enlist, coordinate, and facilitate the work of three task force chairs/co-chairs (lead gift, general solicitation and cultivation) in support of a special solicitation to be conducted among parents seeking $175,000 to fund the final phase of a class room renovation.

TASK

1. Become a major donor in the range of $10,000.

2. Solicit and enlist three task force chairs to conduct cultivation & solicitation programs.

3. Chair all meetings of the campaign committee.

4. Be available to follow up on workers not accomplishing tasks.

Job Description
Parent Special Campaign for Class Room Renovation

CO-CHAIR OF LEADERSHIP GIVING

ROLE

With the support of staff and peers, identify the prospect pool to be solicited for gifts in excess of $1,000. Select, solicit and enlist from among those prospects eight to ten individuals to become lead gift donors, and serve as lead gift workers. Coordinate and support their work.

TASK

1. Become a major donor to the campaign in the range of $7,500 +.

2. Solicit and enlist workers.

3. Host worker orientation event, training to be provided by staff.

4. Support the follow up on assigned workers.

Job Description
Parent Special Campaign for Class Room Renovation

LEAD GIFT WORKER

ROLE

To solicit four to six individuals for gifts in the range of $1,000–$5,000.

TASK

1. Become a donor to the campaign in the range of $1,000+.

2. Attend a two hour prospect rating and orientation session.

3. Develop, with staff and lead gift co-chair, an appropriate cultivation event for assigned prospects.

4. Host cultivation event for assigned prospects.

5. Solicit, in person, each prospect using the suggested "asking" indicated with each prospect.

6. Report all contacts to the development office or lead gift chair upon completion.

7. Return "Call Report Form" and signed pledge card to development office.

Job Description
Parent Special Campaign for Class Room Renovation

CO-CHAIR OF GENERAL APPEAL

ROLE

To see to the effective solicitation of the broad base of remaining parents employing mail and phone solicitations.

TASK

1. Become a major donor to the campaign in the range of $1,000 +.

2. Work with the office to design the "mail appeal" cultivation and solicitation package.

3. Identify with the office parent phonathon worker prospect.

4. Enlist phonathon workers.

5. Host parent phonathon.

Job Description
Parent Special Campaign for Class Room Renovation

CULTIVATION CHAIR

ROLE

Compile a list of questions felt to be in the minds of the parents regarding capital campaign, capital spending, and broader institutional management issues, which could effect their willingness to give. Pose those questions to the proper administration, or board personnel and collate the answers. Work with staff to insure the effective distribution of those answers among the parents prior to their solicitation through written and, wherever possible, personal presentation.

TASK

1. Become a major donor to the campaign in the range of $2,500 +.

2. Work with the campaign committee and the development office to identify and prepare any additional materials felt necessary to support cultivation and solicitation activities.

3. Work with the Development Office to insure that an effective presentation of the facts of the campaign is made at all cultivation events and activities.

SECTION FOUR—

Fitting in the community and living with the school board

22 A new governance to respond to a new day

When a public school board embarks on a serious effort to include private giving as one of the major financial supports of the school program, either the role of the school board must change to encompass the new function or a new governance must be established to carry on the added function. It is enlightening, in this regard, to consider some similarities and differences between a public school board and the board of a private school. The private school board member has inescapably included the role of fund raising in his or her job description.

Public school board members earn a seat on the board by winning an election in which the public at large votes. Over the years, remarkably able and well qualified school board members usually have been elected. Where school board members have been appointed, the results have not been significantly if at all superior. On the other hand, running for election is not to everyone's taste. The candidates must respond to public concerns to win an election and remain conscious of the fact that the voters will judge them in action. This is not all bad, since the major control of the public schools can best be gained by changing school board members. These are public schools.

In selecting public school board members by vote, it is hoped and, for the most part, realized that wise and concerned people will be given office. The qualities that will make the candidate electable are ability to communicate, willingness to ring door bells and shake hands, or to be accessible to as much of the public as possible. Also, the candidate should be wise, capable, dependable and have views that converge with the prevailing views of the community. Political savvy should not be discounted. Personal wealth, however, is not a characteristic that relates to election directly.

The function of the public school board is to set policy for the district. Educational, financial, and management policies are developed, issues resolved, and a superintendent of schools selected. The board must adopt a budget which involves taxing the community. Frequently it must establish a system of gaining public support for budgets or for capital outlays, either of which may be settled by the vote of the people. In some cases the board may obtain funds for the school by setting a tax rate without vote or in securing capital funds through exercise of its legal power or by approval of another agency. Ultimately, the system depends upon the funds raised by taxation. The checks upon the power of the board to raise money lie in the hands of the voters who can refuse to vote the funds or can throw the board out. Funding is a political process, as it should be, that maintains the ultimate control in the hands of the people of the community.

The public school board member traditionally is prepared to deal with the issues of concern to voters. Few would anticipate fund raising from private sources as a regular part of the job.

The member of the board of trustees of a private educational institution, in the nature of the setting, knows that fund raising is a major role of board members. The ability of the board member to play an important role in fund raising is one of the major criteria for selecting the person for the task. While the public school candidate for the board runs the gauntlet of an election to secure a place on the board, the private school candidate is sought out and persuaded to accept membership. Vacancies on the board are filled by the remaining membership as an exercise in self-perpetuation. New members are chosen for their wisdom, their willingness to work, their track record in leadership in the community of the school, and for their personal wealth. The board member must ask for money and can do this best from a position of having given more than he or she is asking for.

The trustee of the private institution has a real concern for the excellence of the school, and acts on policy matters and issues that come before the board. The ultimate test of the success of the board's work is if the constituency of the school supports the institution. In a sense, the parents, graduates, and friends of the school vote with their gifts.

How can the public school board, newly entering into serious solicitation of funds to support public school programs, learn from the practice of the private schools? One of the most widely used approaches is for the public school board to establish a foundation that is empowered to accept tax-free donations to help support the programs of the public schools. This action emulates one function of the private school board by creating an entity that does recognize fund raising as a major concern of its membership. At the same time it recognizes the elected nature of the public school board with its own set of attributes. Since the elected board and the foundation board have the same goal—providing a high quality education to the children in the schools—the policies of the two boards should be convergent. In fact, the two boards will support each other best if they work together at assigning tasks in the light of cooperative planning about the system's future.

A foundation designed to support the work of the public schools can best be established by a volunteer screening committee that takes on the task of establishing the permanent foundation. An interim steering committee composed of volunteers who have shown their stamina and their concern for the schools should be recruited by the school board and the professional administrative staff.

The interim steering committee would be assigned the role of establishing the structure and membership of the foundation. It is they who would undertake the work of raising modest funds to get the foundation chartered and enlisting legal talent to get this task done. They would constitute the temporary staff or give direction to temporary staff or support provided by the school system to get the project underway. A key function of the temporary steering committee would be to identify, cultivate, and enlist the initial board of trustees of the foundation. From then on, the permanent board would be self-perpetuating.

The temporary steering committee should be composed of volunteers who have already shown themselves to be committed to improving the quality of public education in the community. They should be community leaders since they will be asking other community leaders to become permanent board members of the foundation. The temporary committee members must have enthusiasm and time for six months to a year to get the foundation under way. In enlisting temporary committee members the school system should be clear about the demands upon time and the tasks to be done so that those who are invited can judge clearly if they are able to carry out the function.

The members of the steering committee, in searching for board members for the foundation, should develop a list of characteristics that they would expect the new members to meet. The board of the foundation should be made up of recognized community leaders, who themselves will represent a cross-section of the community the public schools serve. Because the board member will have a major responsibility for fund raising, he or she should have a strong potential for personal giving.

The potential for personal giving reflects the truisms about fund raising that before people can ask others to give they must first have given themselves. It is seldom that anyone can ask for more than he or she has already agreed to give. Since the history of fund raising suggests that 80 percent of the dollars in most campaigns come from 10 to 20 percent of the donors, the board must have within its membership those capable of leading the solicitation of that 10 to 20 percent segment of the donors.

The prospective board members should have a track record of willingness to work and capability of getting jobs done. Such people have been involved in successful community service, tending to stick to the job and to follow through until it is finished. The "big name," "no work" volunteer seldom adds more to the board than dead weight.

A deep concern for public education and a willingness to give first priority in time and energy to the foundation are prime requisites.

The process of identifying the prospective members of the board of the foundation involves a broadly based search for possible candidates, a system of evaluation of the nominees or prospective candidates, and the recruitment of the candidates that seem most likely to meet the requirements.

Developing a list of candidates should be based on a broad canvass of the community. This could involve seeking suggestions from such sources as: parent organizations; local clergy; service club officers or other community leaders; former board members; administrators and faculty of the school district; newspaper editors; and radio and TV management.

Once a list of nominees has been assembled a cross reference file of prospects should be compiled to collate information. This is particularly helpful in considering how best to balance the board. Balancing the board implies that the various major constituencies are represented, that the board has its fair share of the strong leaders of the community, and that the board in its membership has access to those who will give. Personal affluence, however, remains as one of the characteristics to be tested.

In evaluating the persons being considered for the post,

the steering committee should avoid politicizing the process. It should make calm and careful judgements to appoint members to the board who will best serve the schools and the community. The evaluation will be acceptable to the extent that it is objective, and based on the facts collected by patient research, not upon hearsay. The process will be better for being formal and systematized. No one should be considered excluded.

One of the key factors in both evaluating and recruiting a prospective board member is a well thought out job description that honestly and clearly describes the role of the foundation and its board. There are two major functions of the foundation. One is to understand the goals of the school system and its long range plans as partners with the professional staff and the elected board. Given a clear understanding of what must be done to achieve these goals, the foundation board should accept, after discussion with the elected board, responsibility for the securing of funds and resources to accomplish the goals assigned to the foundation. These are shared goals where the elected and the foundation board have arrived at consensus and the foundation board has accepted a responsibility for funding some of the planned procedures.

There are some caveats to the procedure discussed above. One is to be patient—to cultivate prospective members of the foundation board and allow them time to consider the job and to grow accustomed to the idea. Membership on the foundation board is arduous but prestigious. It will appeal to many who would never consider running for public office in an election. The steering committee should be prepared for rejections from some who are asked. It is only prudent to have a longer list of suitable candidates than there are seats on the board. Further, the committee should leave a limited number of vacancies on the board. The board itself should have the opportunity of filling out its membership as it sees the need for various individuals or representatives of constituencies that may not be represented.

The relationship between the elected board and the foundation board really cannot be legislated. It is a good working relationship because the common element binding the two boards to work together is the mutual concern for the education of children in the community. Tightly binding the foundation board to the elected board's purposes, practices, and goals would only create a rubber stamp foundation board, which will not attract the kind of people to membership who can make a success of the foundation. The development of common insights and understandings about major goals and the provision of some leeway within which the foundation board can operate on its own is a management task for the administration and board of the public school system.

23 Long range planning: Key link between foundation and board of education

An effective long range planning process will involve members of the board of the foundation and key volunteers in the fund raising program.

Three benefits flow from this action. First, the quality of the long range planning increases with the contribution of board members and volunteers who have already demonstrated a keen interest in education. Second, the fund raising arm of the school system develops clear understandings of the system's traditions, history, accomplishments, weaknesses, and aspirations. It is impossible to plan without knowing where the fund raising campaign is now and where it should go. Third in the planning process, the foundation board and its key volunteers can begin to identify those portions of the long range plan that best fit the fund raising goals and efforts of the foundation. The foundation should maintain the prerogative of setting its own goals and deciding on its tactics and strategies. An effective foundation will test a proposed goal to determine whether it can be met. The foundation will then select a series of possible tasks from among those identified in the long range planning process and test those along with other tasks that it has identified on its own. In this way it can establish its goals and priorities.

Long range planning process

Involving many people in fund raising is necessary to spread understanding of the goals and ways to reach the goals. Fund raising will make the board of education think more broadly and look more carefully at the product to maintain significant public support. Indeed, support must be turned into enthusiasm.

The long range plan nearly always includes some description of where the school system stands today, where it wishes to be tomorrow, and why and how it plans to get from today to tomorrow. A poorly managed system waits. A superior system acts.

This data about the school system, which includes an assessment of strengths and weaknesses and the series of steps that the school system plans to make to improve the quality of education, undergirds the fund raising effort.

The main body of the data report should state truthfully, simply, and clearly the salient material about the current situation. Lengthy tables and details should be reported in an appendix or second volume. This information will be indispensable for volunteers who wish to be convinced on their own. The "doubting Thomas" type often becomes the strongest supporter if he or she is convinced. Since this type is known to be skeptical, its support may be most effective.

Fact finding

A good long range plan includes the following types of data:

1. Demographic data—how many enrolled, changes in the community, birth data, forecasts of enrollment change.
2. The organization of the school system.
3. The programs offered, described in some detail. This could include the number of students in the high school enrolling in higher math, the number in the various advanced placement courses,

and the enrollment in physics at all levels. It could describe the science and mathematics programs in the elementary school and how many students at what level have significant interactions with computers. It could describe the art programs, programs for handicapped children, programs for the gifted and talented, programs in career counseling.

4. Staffing for all these activities should be described, including the actual teacher load, the specialized staff available and their roles, the administrative staff and the provision of non-professional staff to help.

5. A sophisticated school system will probably pay a good deal of attention to the allotment of time to various educational functions, including its programs in athletics and other extra-curricular activities. How students are expected to spend their limited amount of time in school is a simple value system. If a great deal of time is devoted to trivial pursuits and very little to matters significant to students approaching college or work, the differences may prompt a careful inquiry by the school system.

6. The plan will look at the space available to carry on the school's functions, the quality of the space and the way that space is maintained to serve the community in the future. The space available will be analyzed with respect to its ability to accommodate the amount of time students spend at the various activities of the schools. The effectiveness of utilization of space will be derived from comparing the way students use time and the ability of the spaces to accommodate student time.

7. The financial situation of the school system will, of course, be of concern. The background data will show what has been spent on various functions over the years and will show the con-

straints, increasing in number, on spending in the future. Of particular concern, since this is a labor-intensive activity, will be information on staff salaries, including comparisons with other school systems and with other professions. The most significant factor affecting the quality of education is the ability of the system to hire and retain highly effective teachers. If the school system wants to add a highly trained, expert physics teacher, the school system is competing in a very tough market.

8. The management of the school system is another subject on which data probably will be accumulated. The school system's management is generally more understaffed than other businesses and industries. Either the system must develop a corps of highly professional, well qualified teachers who do not need management, or the system will have moderately trained teachers earning lower salaries who need a good deal of supervision to function effectively. It is in this area that much of the effort to improve the quality of instruction will be focused.

Evaluating the educational system

The school system is constantly being evaluated. The evaluation system should range from test results to relative success of graduates, to concern about drop-outs, to graduates' statements of delight with or failure of teachers.

A good long term plan should have a carefully developed system of evaluation. The evaluation should stress the advances students have made. It should compare other systems or standardized test scores with students in the districts. Longitudinal studies of children in the system should be made. The limits of tests should be developed and explained. For example, most standardized tests measure only certain kinds of learning. Students may have ability and potential that go far beyond that which is being measured. No one yet has calibrated the value of a warm smile and a positive attitude toward life. A history of improvement or significant turn around is a good base for fund raising. For systems that test at the top of the scale, the implications for the systematic development of high level thinking skills, creativity, and the like are clear. Student or teacher improvement is certainly good grounds for fund raising.

The long range plan

Within the framework of the plan, the school system, with wide participation by staff, fund raisers, parents, students, and others, should identify steps to be undertaken. These steps will either remedy existing weaknesses, extend previously made advances, or break new ground for the system. This will be the agenda of the school system for a number of years.

A carefully developed plan will have tasks and subtasks, will set these tasks in an order of priority, will assign to the tasks the costs in terms of use of time and money and other resources. It should be possible for the foundation and its volunteers to select the tasks that most closely relate to the capabilities of the foundation, that lie within its resources to accomplish, that arouse the most enthusiasm in the group and community, and that fit into the goals of the foundation.

The framework of the plan

This framework within which the long range plan should function may be the sum of the experiences of the persons creating the plan. It may be a more formal structure. It may be based on research in the field that represents the intellectual framework within which various strategies or subplans exist and are carried out.

One such framework is found in the work of Herbert Walberg ("Improving the Productivity of America's Schools," *Educational Leadership* 41:19–27 May 1984). Walberg analyzed a large number of research studies to determine how the research conclusions affect academic learning. He was asking where resources should be used to get the greatest return in terms of increased academic learning. One area where high returns can be expected is in relating the "alterable curriculum of the home" more closely to that of the school. Advising parents what work habits are to be developed, suggesting parents have a syllabus or some description of the course the children are taking to supplement the school in the home, and similar techniques are described in a *New York Times* article. ("Are the Schools Overlooking Parents?" *New York Times*, December 11, 1985.)

Recognizing and describing the framework of a plan will be a way to develop synergistic relations among tasks so that the sum of the parts, which in this case are all the tasks, will in results be greater than the plan as a whole. Tasks support each other in unintended ways. People learn in the process and become more capable. The plan is more than a bundle of tasks.

Selecting tasks for consideration for private sources funding

The foundation can select out of the bundle of tasks that constitute the long range plan a set of items that seem appealing to its constituency, and within the range of funds it is capable of financing at its current stage of development. Tasks to be undertaken should also generate enthusiasm among its volunteers and respond well when the views of the community are tested.

For example, within the framework of the long range plan, the possibility of improving the relationship between the home and the school curriculum may be one task. The development of materials for parents as an approach to using the home more directly to supplement the schools could be a task in the long range plan. The foundation could consider this task to be funded partly by private money. Extra money may be needed to develop materials, to test the materials in use, and to study the implications of such an approach.

Another example is the necessity of securing or retaining highly professional teachers who can set high standards for learning. Robert Koff, Dean of the School of Education at the State University at Albany, New York, strongly advocates a career ladder in which a small number of highly trained and competent professional teachers would be recruited. Their work would include stimulating the approaches in their subject fields, working with other teachers lower on the career ladders to improve the quality of instruction, and working directly with children. Such teachers would be paid a high professional salary, like the procedures used to endow a teaching post, to attract unusually qualified people to the school.

Again, the foundation could examine the possibility of providing additional funds to endow a post to show its effectiveness or it could provide a series of such teaching opportunities by supplying the funds to pay more than the normal teacher salary.

Linkages

The public school long range plan and its implementation differs from the private school handling of the problem because in the public school two major sources of funds are involved. The public school can use taxation and fund raising to finance necessary projects. As an effective ally, the foundation must be treated carefully to protect its independent decision making and credibility in the community. The foundation should not become the rubber stamp of the public school system.

Long range planning, in which the foundation board and its key volunteers participate fully, is a way to acquire the common understanding of the importance of accomplishing tasks. The linkage is in the common goals and the mutual allocation of tasks. The board of education and the board of the foundation serve the children of the community using different methods to achieve common results.

Index